REA[illegible]ING JOURNAL

This Journal Belongs To:

Journal Timeline:

REVIVE stationery

Reading Journal

ISBN: 978-1-83412-051-5

INDEX

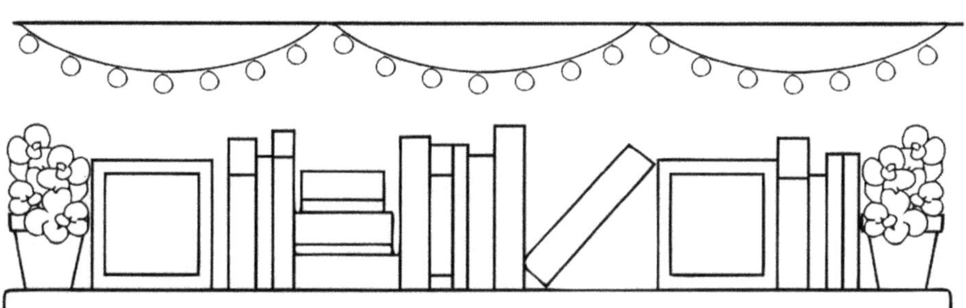

BOOK LOG

BOOK LOG

BOOK LOG

KEEP TRACK OF YOUR BOOKS IN ONE PLACE!

#	TITLE	AUTHOR	SERIES?	RECOMMEND?	ABANDONNED?	RATING (1–5)
			☐	☐	☐	☆☆☆☆☆
			☐	☐	☐	☆☆☆☆☆
			☐	☐	☐	☆☆☆☆☆
			☐	☐	☐	☆☆☆☆☆
			☐	☐	☐	☆☆☆☆☆
			☐	☐	☐	☆☆☆☆☆
			☐	☐	☐	☆☆☆☆☆
			☐	☐	☐	☆☆☆☆☆
			☐	☐	☐	☆☆☆☆☆
			☐	☐	☐	☆☆☆☆☆
			☐	☐	☐	☆☆☆☆☆
			☐	☐	☐	☆☆☆☆☆
			☐	☐	☐	☆☆☆☆☆
			☐	☐	☐	☆☆☆☆☆
			☐	☐	☐	☆☆☆☆☆
			☐	☐	☐	☆☆☆☆☆
			☐	☐	☐	☆☆☆☆☆
			☐	☐	☐	☆☆☆☆☆
			☐	☐	☐	☆☆☆☆☆
			☐	☐	☐	☆☆☆☆☆
			☐	☐	☐	☆☆☆☆☆
			☐	☐	☐	☆☆☆☆☆

BOOK LOG

KEEP TRACK OF YOUR BOOKS IN ONE PLACE!

#	TITLE	AUTHOR	SERIES?	RECOMMEND?	ABANDONNED?	RATING (1-5)
			☐	☐	☐	☆☆☆☆☆
			☐	☐	☐	☆☆☆☆☆
			☐	☐	☐	☆☆☆☆☆
			☐	☐	☐	☆☆☆☆☆
			☐	☐	☐	☆☆☆☆☆
			☐	☐	☐	☆☆☆☆☆
			☐	☐	☐	☆☆☆☆☆
			☐	☐	☐	☆☆☆☆☆
			☐	☐	☐	☆☆☆☆☆
			☐	☐	☐	☆☆☆☆☆
			☐	☐	☐	☆☆☆☆☆
			☐	☐	☐	☆☆☆☆☆
			☐	☐	☐	☆☆☆☆☆
			☐	☐	☐	☆☆☆☆☆
			☐	☐	☐	☆☆☆☆☆
			☐	☐	☐	☆☆☆☆☆
			☐	☐	☐	☆☆☆☆☆
			☐	☐	☐	☆☆☆☆☆
			☐	☐	☐	☆☆☆☆☆
			☐	☐	☐	☆☆☆☆☆
			☐	☐	☐	☆☆☆☆☆
			☐	☐	☐	☆☆☆☆☆

BOOK LOG

KEEP TRACK OF YOUR BOOKS IN ONE PLACE!

#	TITLE	AUTHOR	SERIES?	RECOMMEND?	ABANDONNED?	RATING (1-5)
			☐	☐	☐	☆☆☆☆☆
			☐	☐	☐	☆☆☆☆☆
			☐	☐	☐	☆☆☆☆☆
			☐	☐	☐	☆☆☆☆☆
			☐	☐	☐	☆☆☆☆☆
			☐	☐	☐	☆☆☆☆☆
			☐	☐	☐	☆☆☆☆☆
			☐	☐	☐	☆☆☆☆☆
			☐	☐	☐	☆☆☆☆☆
			☐	☐	☐	☆☆☆☆☆
			☐	☐	☐	☆☆☆☆☆
			☐	☐	☐	☆☆☆☆☆
			☐	☐	☐	☆☆☆☆☆
			☐	☐	☐	☆☆☆☆☆
			☐	☐	☐	☆☆☆☆☆
			☐	☐	☐	☆☆☆☆☆
			☐	☐	☐	☆☆☆☆☆
			☐	☐	☐	☆☆☆☆☆
			☐	☐	☐	☆☆☆☆☆
			☐	☐	☐	☆☆☆☆☆
			☐	☐	☐	☆☆☆☆☆
			☐	☐	☐	☆☆☆☆☆

BOOK LOG

KEEP TRACK OF YOUR BOOKS IN ONE PLACE!

#	TITLE	AUTHOR	SERIES?	RECOMMEND?	ABANDONNED?	RATING (1-5)
			☐	☐	☐	☆☆☆☆☆
			☐	☐	☐	☆☆☆☆☆
			☐	☐	☐	☆☆☆☆☆
			☐	☐	☐	☆☆☆☆☆
			☐	☐	☐	☆☆☆☆☆
			☐	☐	☐	☆☆☆☆☆
			☐	☐	☐	☆☆☆☆☆
			☐	☐	☐	☆☆☆☆☆
			☐	☐	☐	☆☆☆☆☆
			☐	☐	☐	☆☆☆☆☆
			☐	☐	☐	☆☆☆☆☆
			☐	☐	☐	☆☆☆☆☆
			☐	☐	☐	☆☆☆☆☆
			☐	☐	☐	☆☆☆☆☆
			☐	☐	☐	☆☆☆☆☆
			☐	☐	☐	☆☆☆☆☆
			☐	☐	☐	☆☆☆☆☆
			☐	☐	☐	☆☆☆☆☆
			☐	☐	☐	☆☆☆☆☆
			☐	☐	☐	☆☆☆☆☆
			☐	☐	☐	☆☆☆☆☆
			☐	☐	☐	☆☆☆☆☆

BOOK LOG

KEEP TRACK OF YOUR BOOKS IN ONE PLACE!

#	TITLE	AUTHOR	SERIES?	RECOMMEND?	ABANDONNED?	RATING (1-5)
			☐	☐	☐	☆☆☆☆☆
			☐	☐	☐	☆☆☆☆☆
			☐	☐	☐	☆☆☆☆☆
			☐	☐	☐	☆☆☆☆☆
			☐	☐	☐	☆☆☆☆☆
			☐	☐	☐	☆☆☆☆☆
			☐	☐	☐	☆☆☆☆☆
			☐	☐	☐	☆☆☆☆☆
			☐	☐	☐	☆☆☆☆☆
			☐	☐	☐	☆☆☆☆☆
			☐	☐	☐	☆☆☆☆☆
			☐	☐	☐	☆☆☆☆☆
			☐	☐	☐	☆☆☆☆☆
			☐	☐	☐	☆☆☆☆☆
			☐	☐	☐	☆☆☆☆☆
			☐	☐	☐	☆☆☆☆☆
			☐	☐	☐	☆☆☆☆☆
			☐	☐	☐	☆☆☆☆☆
			☐	☐	☐	☆☆☆☆☆
			☐	☐	☐	☆☆☆☆☆
			☐	☐	☐	☆☆☆☆☆
			☐	☐	☐	☆☆☆☆☆

BOOK LOG

KEEP TRACK OF YOUR BOOKS IN ONE PLACE!

#	TITLE	AUTHOR	SERIES?	RECOMMEND?	ABANDONNED?	RATING (1–5)
			☐	☐	☐	☆☆☆☆☆
			☐	☐	☐	☆☆☆☆☆
			☐	☐	☐	☆☆☆☆☆
			☐	☐	☐	☆☆☆☆☆
			☐	☐	☐	☆☆☆☆☆
			☐	☐	☐	☆☆☆☆☆
			☐	☐	☐	☆☆☆☆☆
			☐	☐	☐	☆☆☆☆☆
			☐	☐	☐	☆☆☆☆☆
			☐	☐	☐	☆☆☆☆☆
			☐	☐	☐	☆☆☆☆☆
			☐	☐	☐	☆☆☆☆☆
			☐	☐	☐	☆☆☆☆☆
			☐	☐	☐	☆☆☆☆☆
			☐	☐	☐	☆☆☆☆☆
			☐	☐	☐	☆☆☆☆☆
			☐	☐	☐	☆☆☆☆☆
			☐	☐	☐	☆☆☆☆☆
			☐	☐	☐	☆☆☆☆☆
			☐	☐	☐	☆☆☆☆☆
			☐	☐	☐	☆☆☆☆☆
			☐	☐	☐	☆☆☆☆☆

BOOK LOG

KEEP TRACK OF YOUR BOOKS IN ONE PLACE!

#	TITLE	AUTHOR	SERIES?	RECOMMEND?	ABANDONNED?	RATING (1-5)
			☐	☐	☐	☆☆☆☆☆
			☐	☐	☐	☆☆☆☆☆
			☐	☐	☐	☆☆☆☆☆
			☐	☐	☐	☆☆☆☆☆
			☐	☐	☐	☆☆☆☆☆
			☐	☐	☐	☆☆☆☆☆
			☐	☐	☐	☆☆☆☆☆
			☐	☐	☐	☆☆☆☆☆
			☐	☐	☐	☆☆☆☆☆
			☐	☐	☐	☆☆☆☆☆
			☐	☐	☐	☆☆☆☆☆
			☐	☐	☐	☆☆☆☆☆
			☐	☐	☐	☆☆☆☆☆
			☐	☐	☐	☆☆☆☆☆
			☐	☐	☐	☆☆☆☆☆
			☐	☐	☐	☆☆☆☆☆
			☐	☐	☐	☆☆☆☆☆
			☐	☐	☐	☆☆☆☆☆
			☐	☐	☐	☆☆☆☆☆
			☐	☐	☐	☆☆☆☆☆
			☐	☐	☐	☆☆☆☆☆
			☐	☐	☐	☆☆☆☆☆

BOOK LOG

KEEP TRACK OF YOUR BOOKS IN ONE PLACE!

#	TITLE	AUTHOR	SERIES?	RECOMMEND?	ABANDONNED?	RATING (1-5)
			☐	☐	☐	☆☆☆☆☆
			☐	☐	☐	☆☆☆☆☆
			☐	☐	☐	☆☆☆☆☆
			☐	☐	☐	☆☆☆☆☆
			☐	☐	☐	☆☆☆☆☆
			☐	☐	☐	☆☆☆☆☆
			☐	☐	☐	☆☆☆☆☆
			☐	☐	☐	☆☆☆☆☆
			☐	☐	☐	☆☆☆☆☆
			☐	☐	☐	☆☆☆☆☆
			☐	☐	☐	☆☆☆☆☆
			☐	☐	☐	☆☆☆☆☆
			☐	☐	☐	☆☆☆☆☆
			☐	☐	☐	☆☆☆☆☆
			☐	☐	☐	☆☆☆☆☆
			☐	☐	☐	☆☆☆☆☆
			☐	☐	☐	☆☆☆☆☆
			☐	☐	☐	☆☆☆☆☆
			☐	☐	☐	☆☆☆☆☆
			☐	☐	☐	☆☆☆☆☆
			☐	☐	☐	☆☆☆☆☆
			☐	☐	☐	☆☆☆☆☆

FAVORITE BOOKS

FAVORITE BOOKS

FAVORITE BOOKS

EASILY FIND THOSE HIDDEN GEMS AGAIN!

#	TITLE	AUTHOR	NOTES

FAVORITE BOOKS

EASILY FIND THOSE HIDDEN GEMS AGAIN!

#	TITLE	AUTHOR	NOTES

FAVORITE BOOKS

EASILY FIND THOSE HIDDEN GEMS AGAIN!

#	TITLE	AUTHOR	NOTES

FAVORITE BOOKS

EASILY FIND THOSE HIDDEN GEMS AGAIN!

#	TITLE	AUTHOR	NOTES

FAVORITE BOOKS

EASILY FIND THOSE HIDDEN GEMS AGAIN!

#	TITLE	AUTHOR	NOTES

FAVORITE BOOKS

EASILY FIND THOSE HIDDEN GEMS AGAIN!

#	TITLE	AUTHOR	NOTES

FAVORITE QUOTES

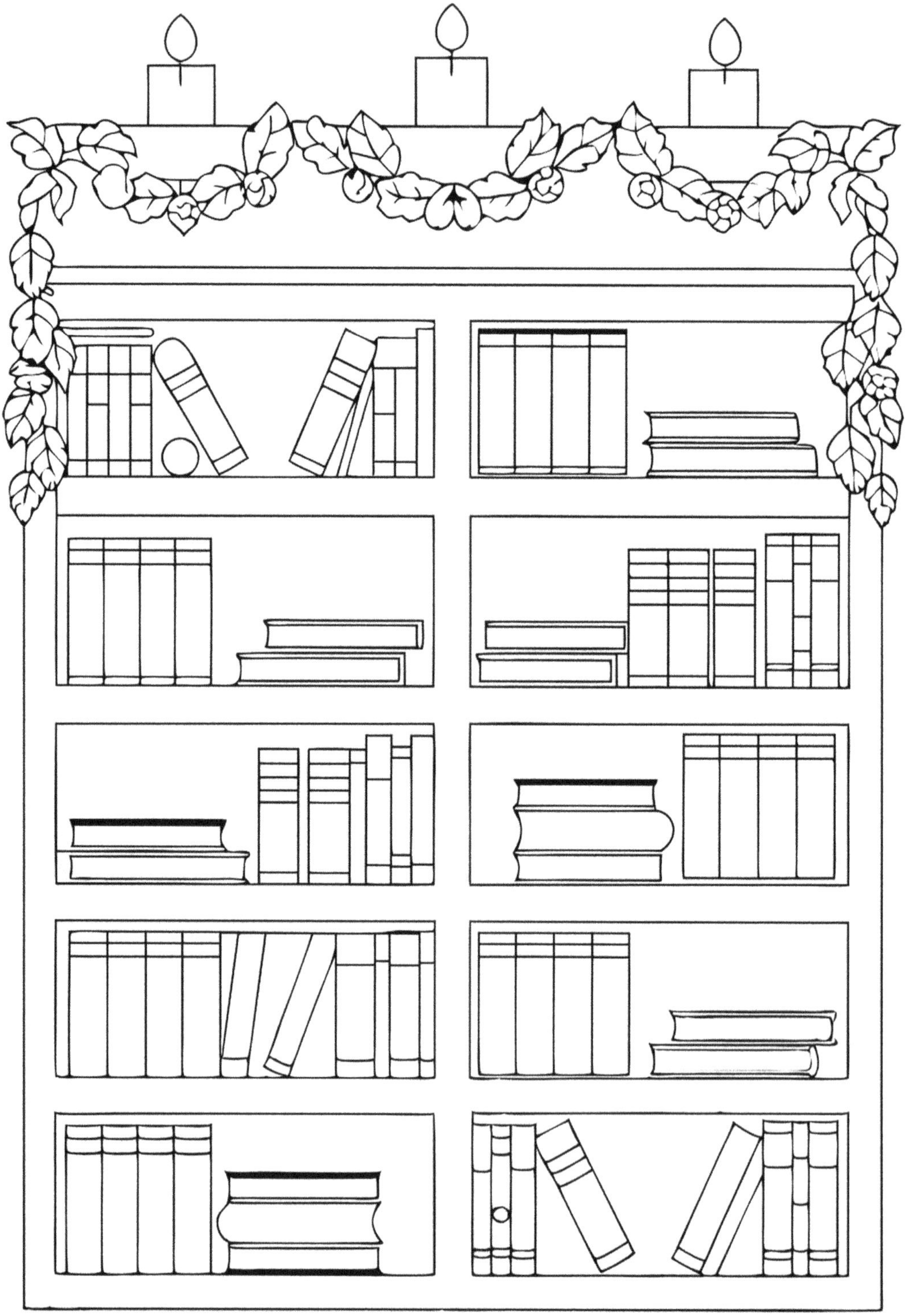

FAVORITE QUOTES

FAVORITE QUOTES

NEVER LOSE THOSE SPECIAL MOMENTS

#	BOOK TITLE/SERIES TITLE	AUTHOR

QUOTE(S)

#	BOOK TITLE/SERIES TITLE	AUTHOR

QUOTE(S)

#	BOOK TITLE/SERIES TITLE	AUTHOR

QUOTE(S)

#	BOOK TITLE/SERIES TITLE	AUTHOR

QUOTE(S)

FAVORITE QUOTES

NEVER LOSE THOSE SPECIAL MOMENTS

#	BOOK TITLE/SERIES TITLE	AUTHOR

QUOTE(S)

#	BOOK TITLE/SERIES TITLE	AUTHOR

QUOTE(S)

#	BOOK TITLE/SERIES TITLE	AUTHOR

QUOTE(S)

#	BOOK TITLE/SERIES TITLE	AUTHOR

QUOTE(S)

FAVORITE QUOTES

NEVER LOSE THOSE SPECIAL MOMENTS

#	BOOK TITLE/SERIES TITLE	AUTHOR
QUOTE(S)		

#	BOOK TITLE/SERIES TITLE	AUTHOR
QUOTE(S)		

#	BOOK TITLE/SERIES TITLE	AUTHOR
QUOTE(S)		

#	BOOK TITLE/SERIES TITLE	AUTHOR
QUOTE(S)		

FAVORITE QUOTES

NEVER LOSE THOSE SPECIAL MOMENTS

#	BOOK TITLE/SERIES TITLE	AUTHOR

QUOTE(S)

#	BOOK TITLE/SERIES TITLE	AUTHOR

QUOTE(S)

#	BOOK TITLE/SERIES TITLE	AUTHOR

QUOTE(S)

#	BOOK TITLE/SERIES TITLE	AUTHOR

QUOTE(S)

FAVORITE QUOTES

NEVER LOSE THOSE SPECIAL MOMENTS

#	BOOK TITLE/SERIES TITLE	AUTHOR

QUOTE(S)

#	BOOK TITLE/SERIES TITLE	AUTHOR

QUOTE(S)

#	BOOK TITLE/SERIES TITLE	AUTHOR

QUOTE(S)

#	BOOK TITLE/SERIES TITLE	AUTHOR

QUOTE(S)

FAVORITE QUOTES

NEVER LOSE THOSE SPECIAL MOMENTS

#	BOOK TITLE/SERIES TITLE	AUTHOR
QUOTE(S)		

#	BOOK TITLE/SERIES TITLE	AUTHOR
QUOTE(S)		

#	BOOK TITLE/SERIES TITLE	AUTHOR
QUOTE(S)		

#	BOOK TITLE/SERIES TITLE	AUTHOR
QUOTE(S)		

READING TRACKER

READING TRACKER

READING TRACKER

COLOR THE STORY OF YOUR READING LIFE!

DAY	JAN	FEB	MAR	APR	MAY	JUN
1						
2						
3						
4						
5						
6						
7						
8						
9						
10						
11						
12						
13						
14						
15						
16						
17						
18						
19						
20						
21						
22						
23						
24						
25						
26						
27						
28						
29						
30						
31						

- ☐ 0-15 PAGES
- ☐ 15-30 PAGES
- ☐ 30-45 PAGES
- ☐ 45-60 PAGES
- ☐ 60-75 PAGES
- ☐ 75-90 PAGES
- ☐ 90-105 PAGES
- ☐ 105-120 PAGES
- ☐ 120+ PAGES

READING TRACKER

COLOR THE STORY OF YOUR READING LIFE!

DAY	JUL	AUG	SEPT	OCT	NOV	DEC
1						
2						
3						
4						
5						
6						
7						
8						
9						
10						
11						
12						
13						
14						
15						
16						
17						
18						
19						
20						
21						
22						
23						
24						
25						
26						
27						
28						
29						
30						
31						

- ☐ 0-15 PAGES
- ☐ 15-30 PAGES
- ☐ 30-45 PAGES
- ☐ 45-60 PAGES
- ☐ 60-75 PAGES
- ☐ 75-90 PAGES
- ☐ 90-105 PAGES
- ☐ 105-120 PAGES
- ☐ 120+ PAGES

CHALLENGES

CHALLENGES

BOOK BINGO

BINGO YOUR WAY THROUGH THE BOOKSHELF!

SET IN A FOREIGN LAND	TRUE CRIME	AWARD WINNER	A COLOR IN THE TITLE	UNDER 200 PAGES
YOUR FAVORITE GENRE	NEW-TO-YOU CULTURE	ANIMAL ON THE COVER	MADE INTO A SHOW	FOREIGN AUTHOR
ONE-WORD TITLE	NON-FICTION	PUBLISHED THIS YEAR	A SEQUEL	SET IN YOUR REGION
FANTASY BOOK	A FACE ON THE COVER	A CLASSIC	HISTORIC SETTING	NEW-TO-YOU GENRE
MADE INTO A MOVIE	OVER 500 PAGES	NEW-TO-YOU AUTHOR	YOUR CHOICE	NUMBER IN THE TITLE

ALPHABET CHALLENGE

YOUR READING QUEST STARTS NOW!

A
B
C
D
E
F
G
H
I
J
K
L
M
N
O
P
Q
R
S
T
U
V
W
X
Y
Z

100 BOOK CHALLENGE

100 BOOKS? CHALLENGE ACCEPTED!

100 BOOK CHALLENGE

TURN PAGES, WIN BRAGGING RIGHTS!

100 BOOK CHALLENGE

ONE BOOK CLOSER TO VICTORY!

100 BOOK CHALLENGE

READ IT. CHECK IT. CONQUER THE CHALLENGE!

BOOK OF THE MONTH

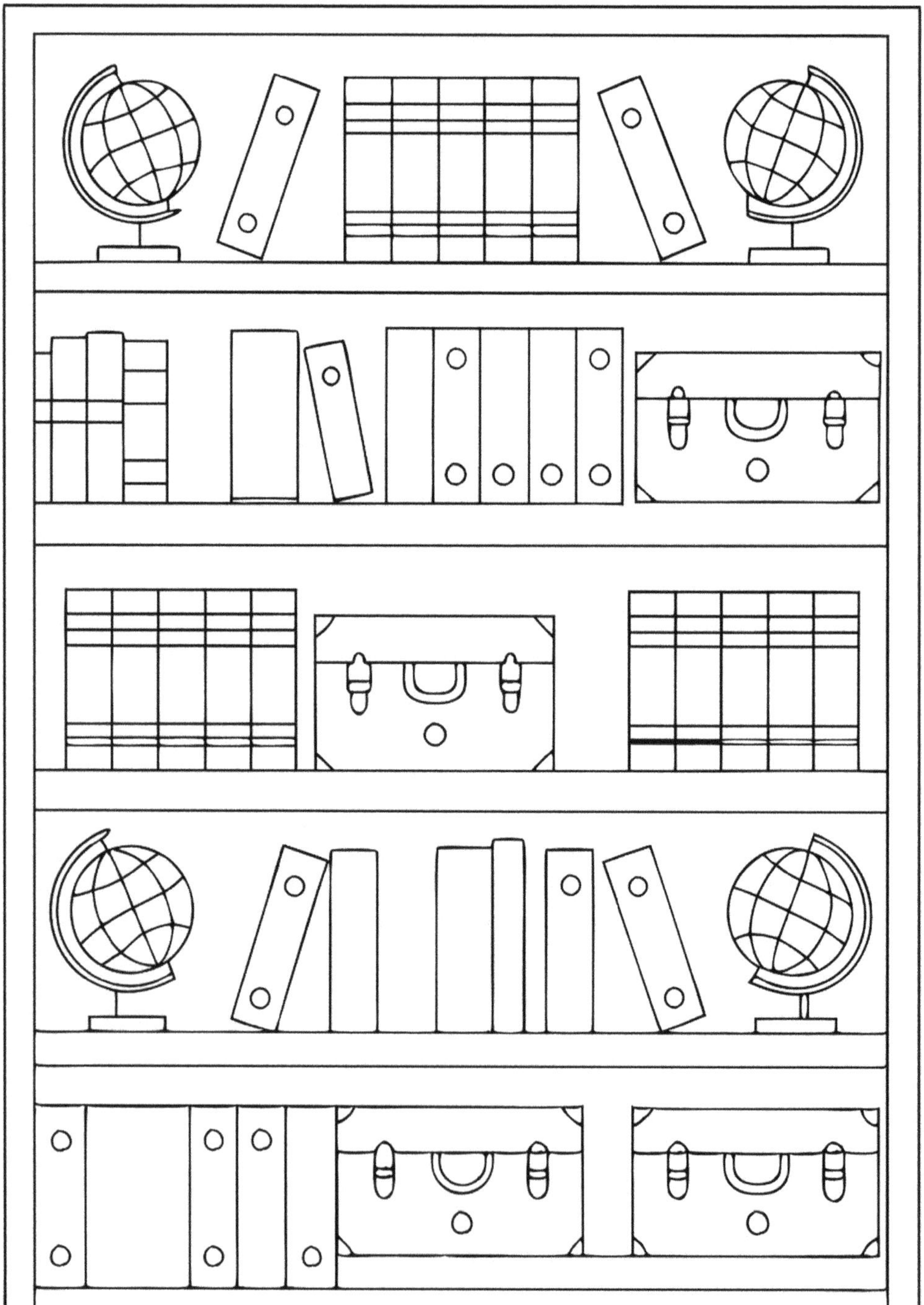

BOOK OF THE MONTH

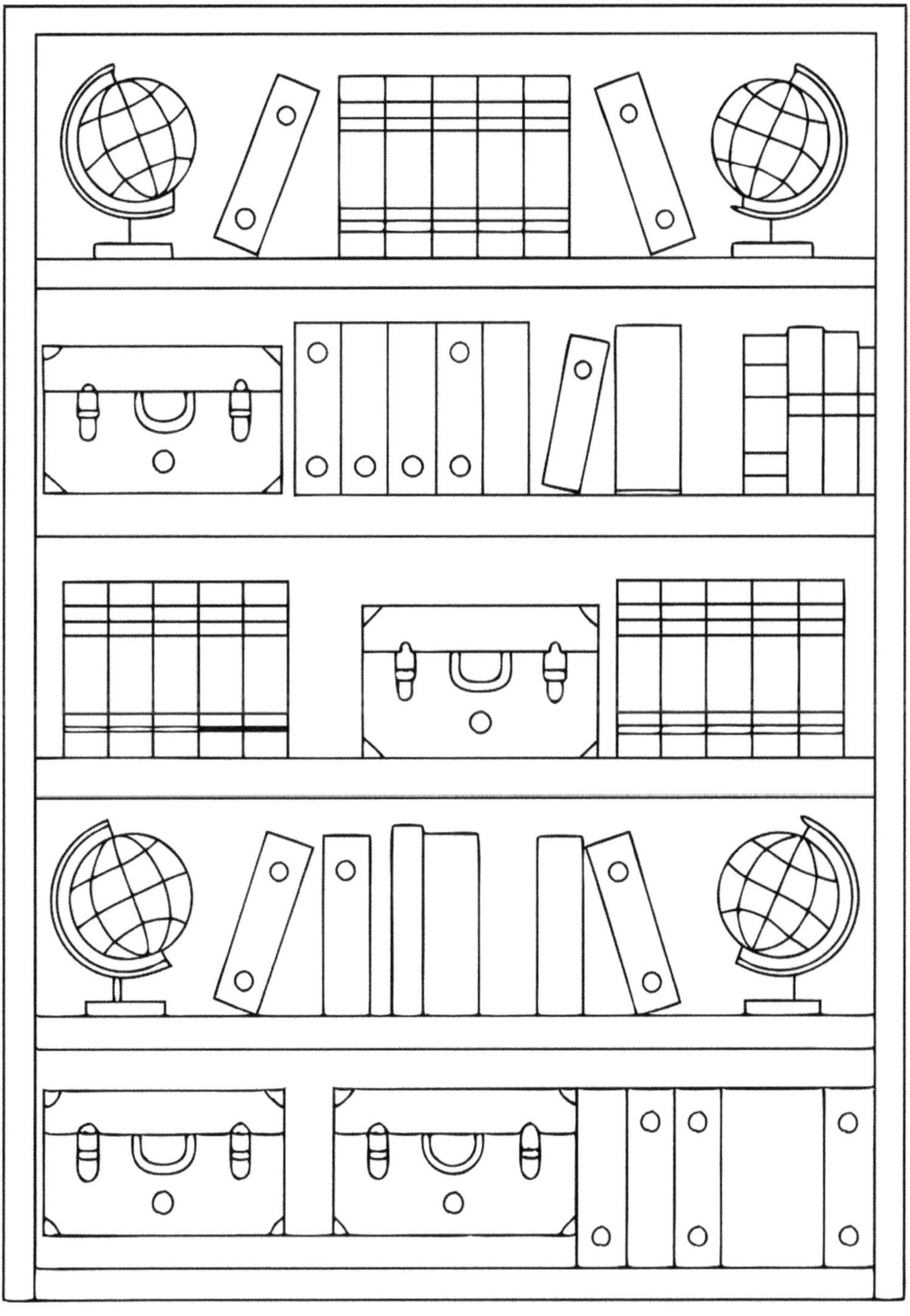

BOOK OF THE MONTH

A YEAR OF PAGES, A YEAR OF POSSIBILITIES.

JANUARY

TITLE

AUTHOR

GENRE

QUOTE

FEBRUARY

TITLE

AUTHOR

GENRE

QUOTE

MARCH

TITLE

AUTHOR

GENRE

QUOTE

BOOK OF THE MONTH

BOOKED EVERY MONTH, INSPIRED ALL YEAR.

APRIL

TITLE

AUTHOR

GENRE

QUOTE

MAY

TITLE

AUTHOR

GENRE

QUOTE

JUNE

TITLE

AUTHOR

GENRE

QUOTE

BOOK OF THE MONTH

12 MONTHS. 12 BOOKS.
ONE INCREDIBLE READING JOURNEY.

JULY

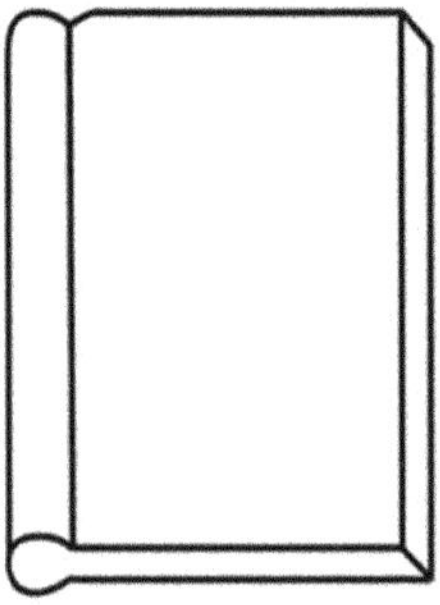

TITLE

AUTHOR

GENRE

QUOTE

AUGUST

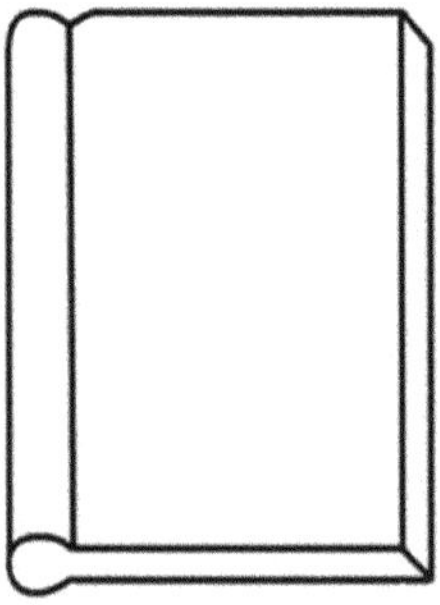

TITLE

AUTHOR

GENRE

QUOTE

SEPTEMBER

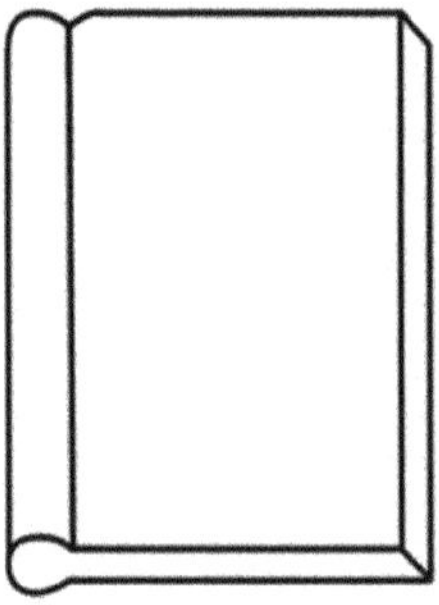

TITLE

AUTHOR

GENRE

QUOTE

BOOK OF THE MONTH

EVERY MONTH HAD A STORY—
TOGETHER THEY TOLD A YEAR.

OCTOBER

TITLE

AUTHOR

GENRE

QUOTE

NOVEMBER

TITLE

AUTHOR

GENRE

QUOTE

DECEMBER

TITLE

AUTHOR

GENRE

QUOTE

BOOK OF THE YEAR

BOOK OF THE YEAR

BOOK OF THE YEAR

TWELVE MONTHS. TWELVE STORIES.
ONE EPIC YEAR OF READING.

JANUARY

FEBRUARY

MARCH

APRIL

MAY

JUNE

JULY

AUGUST

SEPTEMBER

OCTOBER

NOVEMBER

DECEMBER

BOOK OF THE YEAR

THE READ THAT LEFT A MARK—BOOK OF THE YEAR!

TITLE

AUTHOR

GENRE

QUOTE

BOOK REVIEWS

BOOK REVIEWS

BOOK REVIEW

#

TITLE	AUTHOR

☐ FICTION
☐ NON-FICTION

GENRE ____________

FIRST PUBLISHED ____________

NEW-TO-ME AUTHOR? ☐ YES ☐ NO

PAGE COUNT ______

FORMAT ☐ HARDCOVER ☐ PAPERBACK ☐ EBOOK ☐ AUDIOBOOK

SOURCE ☐ BOUGHT ☐ BORROWED ☐ GIFTED ☐ OTHER ______

STARTED BOOK

____

FINISHED BOOK

____

WOULD RECOMMEND?

☐ YES ☐ NO ☐ MAYBE

RECOMMEND TO

____

WOULD READ AGAIN?

☐ YES ☐ NO ☐ MAYBE

WOULD READ OTHER AUTHOR'S BOOKS?

☐ YES ☐ NO ☐ MAYBE

BOOK RATING

EASE OF READING

☆☆☆☆☆

CHARACTERS

☆☆☆☆☆

PLOT

☆☆☆☆☆

ENJOYABILITY

☆☆☆☆☆

OVERALL RATING

☆☆☆☆☆

DESCRIBE THE BOOK IN ONE SENTENCE

____

WHAT DREW ME TO THIS BOOK?

____

QUOTES/FAVORITE PASSAGES

____

____

____

____

____

____

REVIEW

____

____

____

____

____

____

____

____

BOOK REVIEW

#

TITLE	AUTHOR

☐ FICTION
☐ NON-FICTION

GENRE

FIRST PUBLISHED

NEW-TO-ME AUTHOR?
☐ YES ☐ NO

PAGE COUNT

FORMAT ☐ HARDCOVER ☐ PAPERBACK ☐ EBOOK ☐ AUDIOBOOK

SOURCE ☐ BOUGHT ☐ BORROWED ☐ GIFTED ☐ OTHER

DESCRIBE THE BOOK IN ONE SENTENCE

WHAT DREW ME TO THIS BOOK?

QUOTES/FAVORITE PASSAGES

REVIEW

STARTED BOOK

FINISHED BOOK

WOULD RECOMMEND?
☐ YES ☐ NO ☐ MAYBE

RECOMMEND TO

WOULD READ AGAIN?
☐ YES ☐ NO ☐ MAYBE

WOULD READ OTHER AUTHOR'S BOOKS?
☐ YES ☐ NO ☐ MAYBE

BOOK RATING

EASE OF READING
☆☆☆☆☆

CHARACTERS
☆☆☆☆☆

PLOT
☆☆☆☆☆

ENJOYABILITY
☆☆☆☆☆

OVERALL RATING
☆☆☆☆☆

BOOK REVIEW

#

TITLE	AUTHOR

☐ FICTION
☐ NON-FICTION

GENRE ______

FIRST PUBLISHED ______

NEW-TO-ME AUTHOR? ☐ YES ☐ NO

PAGE COUNT ______

FORMAT ☐ HARDCOVER ☐ PAPERBACK ☐ EBOOK ☐ AUDIOBOOK

SOURCE ☐ BOUGHT ☐ BORROWED ☐ GIFTED ☐ OTHER ______

STARTED BOOK ______

FINISHED BOOK ______

WOULD RECOMMEND?
☐ YES ☐ NO ☐ MAYBE

RECOMMEND TO ______

WOULD READ AGAIN?
☐ YES ☐ NO ☐ MAYBE

WOULD READ OTHER AUTHOR'S BOOKS?
☐ YES ☐ NO ☐ MAYBE

BOOK RATING

EASE OF READING
☆☆☆☆☆

CHARACTERS
☆☆☆☆☆

PLOT
☆☆☆☆☆

ENJOYABILITY
☆☆☆☆☆

OVERALL RATING
☆☆☆☆☆

DESCRIBE THE BOOK IN ONE SENTENCE
______

WHAT DREW ME TO THIS BOOK?
______

QUOTES/FAVORITE PASSAGES
______

REVIEW
______

BOOK REVIEW

\#

TITLE	AUTHOR

☐ FICTION
☐ NON-FICTION

GENRE

FIRST PUBLISHED

NEW-TO-ME AUTHOR?
☐ YES ☐ NO

PAGE COUNT

FORMAT ☐ HARDCOVER ☐ PAPERBACK ☐ EBOOK ☐ AUDIOBOOK

SOURCE ☐ BOUGHT ☐ BORROWED ☐ GIFTED ☐ OTHER ______

DESCRIBE THE BOOK IN ONE SENTENCE

WHAT DREW ME TO THIS BOOK?

QUOTES/FAVORITE PASSAGES

REVIEW

STARTED BOOK

FINISHED BOOK

WOULD RECOMMEND?
☐ YES ☐ NO ☐ MAYBE

RECOMMEND TO

WOULD READ AGAIN?
☐ YES ☐ NO ☐ MAYBE

WOULD READ OTHER AUTHOR'S BOOKS?
☐ YES ☐ NO ☐ MAYBE

BOOK RATING

EASE OF READING
☆☆☆☆☆

CHARACTERS
☆☆☆☆☆

PLOT
☆☆☆☆☆

ENJOYABILITY
☆☆☆☆☆

OVERALL RATING
☆☆☆☆☆

BOOK REVIEW

#

TITLE	AUTHOR

☐ FICTION
☐ NON-FICTION

GENRE ____________

FIRST PUBLISHED ____________

NEW-TO-ME AUTHOR?
☐ YES ☐ NO

PAGE COUNT ________

FORMAT ☐ HARDCOVER ☐ PAPERBACK ☐ EBOOK ☐ AUDIOBOOK

SOURCE ☐ BOUGHT ☐ BORROWED ☐ GIFTED ☐ OTHER ________

STARTED BOOK ____________

FINISHED BOOK ____________

WOULD RECOMMEND?
☐ YES ☐ NO ☐ MAYBE

RECOMMEND TO ____________

WOULD READ AGAIN?
☐ YES ☐ NO ☐ MAYBE

WOULD READ OTHER AUTHOR'S BOOKS?
☐ YES ☐ NO ☐ MAYBE

BOOK RATING

EASE OF READING
☆☆☆☆☆

CHARACTERS
☆☆☆☆☆

PLOT
☆☆☆☆☆

ENJOYABILITY
☆☆☆☆☆

OVERALL RATING
☆☆☆☆☆

DESCRIBE THE BOOK IN ONE SENTENCE

WHAT DREW ME TO THIS BOOK?

QUOTES/FAVORITE PASSAGES

REVIEW

BOOK REVIEW

#
___

TITLE	AUTHOR

☐ FICTION
☐ NON-FICTION

GENRE ______________________

FIRST PUBLISHED ______________

NEW-TO-ME AUTHOR? ☐ YES ☐ NO

PAGE COUNT ________

FORMAT ☐ HARDCOVER ☐ PAPERBACK ☐ EBOOK ☐ AUDIOBOOK

SOURCE ☐ BOUGHT ☐ BORROWED ☐ GIFTED ☐ OTHER ________

DESCRIBE THE BOOK IN ONE SENTENCE

____

WHAT DREW ME TO THIS BOOK?

____

QUOTES/FAVORITE PASSAGES

____

____

____

____

____

____

REVIEW

____

____

____

____

____

____

____

____

STARTED BOOK

____

FINISHED BOOK

____

WOULD RECOMMEND?

☐ YES ☐ NO ☐ MAYBE

RECOMMEND TO

____

WOULD READ AGAIN?

☐ YES ☐ NO ☐ MAYBE

WOULD READ OTHER AUTHOR'S BOOKS?

☐ YES ☐ NO ☐ MAYBE

BOOK RATING

EASE OF READING

☆☆☆☆☆

CHARACTERS

☆☆☆☆☆

PLOT

☆☆☆☆☆

ENJOYABILITY

☆☆☆☆☆

OVERALL RATING

☆☆☆☆☆

BOOK REVIEW

#

TITLE	AUTHOR

☐ FICTION
☐ NON-FICTION

GENRE

FIRST PUBLISHED

NEW-TO-ME AUTHOR? ☐ YES ☐ NO

PAGE COUNT

FORMAT ☐ HARDCOVER ☐ PAPERBACK ☐ EBOOK ☐ AUDIOBOOK

SOURCE ☐ BOUGHT ☐ BORROWED ☐ GIFTED ☐ OTHER

STARTED BOOK

FINISHED BOOK

WOULD RECOMMEND?
☐ YES ☐ NO ☐ MAYBE

RECOMMEND TO

WOULD READ AGAIN?
☐ YES ☐ NO ☐ MAYBE

WOULD READ OTHER AUTHOR'S BOOKS?
☐ YES ☐ NO ☐ MAYBE

BOOK RATING

EASE OF READING
☆☆☆☆☆

CHARACTERS
☆☆☆☆☆

PLOT
☆☆☆☆☆

ENJOYABILITY
☆☆☆☆☆

OVERALL RATING
☆☆☆☆☆

DESCRIBE THE BOOK IN ONE SENTENCE

WHAT DREW ME TO THIS BOOK?

QUOTES/FAVORITE PASSAGES

REVIEW

BOOK REVIEW

#

TITLE	AUTHOR

☐ FICTION
☐ NON-FICTION

GENRE

FIRST PUBLISHED

NEW-TO-ME AUTHOR?
☐ YES ☐ NO

PAGE COUNT

FORMAT ☐ HARDCOVER ☐ PAPERBACK ☐ EBOOK ☐ AUDIOBOOK

SOURCE ☐ BOUGHT ☐ BORROWED ☐ GIFTED ☐ OTHER ______

DESCRIBE THE BOOK IN ONE SENTENCE

WHAT DREW ME TO THIS BOOK?

QUOTES/FAVORITE PASSAGES

REVIEW

STARTED BOOK

FINISHED BOOK

WOULD RECOMMEND?
☐ YES ☐ NO ☐ MAYBE

RECOMMEND TO

WOULD READ AGAIN?
☐ YES ☐ NO ☐ MAYBE

WOULD READ OTHER AUTHOR'S BOOKS?
☐ YES ☐ NO ☐ MAYBE

BOOK RATING

EASE OF READING
☆☆☆☆☆

CHARACTERS
☆☆☆☆☆

PLOT
☆☆☆☆☆

ENJOYABILITY
☆☆☆☆☆

OVERALL RATING
☆☆☆☆☆

BOOK REVIEW

#

TITLE	AUTHOR

☐ FICTION
☐ NON-FICTION

GENRE ____________

FIRST PUBLISHED ____________

NEW-TO-ME AUTHOR?
☐ YES ☐ NO

PAGE COUNT ________

FORMAT ☐ HARDCOVER ☐ PAPERBACK ☐ EBOOK ☐ AUDIOBOOK

SOURCE ☐ BOUGHT ☐ BORROWED ☐ GIFTED ☐ OTHER ________

STARTED BOOK
____

FINISHED BOOK
____

WOULD RECOMMEND?
☐ YES ☐ NO ☐ MAYBE

RECOMMEND TO
____

WOULD READ AGAIN?
☐ YES ☐ NO ☐ MAYBE

WOULD READ OTHER AUTHOR'S BOOKS?
☐ YES ☐ NO ☐ MAYBE

BOOK RATING

EASE OF READING
☆☆☆☆☆

CHARACTERS
☆☆☆☆☆

PLOT
☆☆☆☆☆

ENJOYABILITY
☆☆☆☆☆

OVERALL RATING
☆☆☆☆☆

DESCRIBE THE BOOK IN ONE SENTENCE
____

WHAT DREW ME TO THIS BOOK?
____

QUOTES/FAVORITE PASSAGES
____

REVIEW
____

BOOK REVIEW

#

TITLE	AUTHOR

☐ FICTION
☐ NON-FICTION

GENRE ______

FIRST PUBLISHED ______

NEW-TO-ME AUTHOR?
☐ YES ☐ NO

PAGE COUNT ______

FORMAT ☐ HARDCOVER ☐ PAPERBACK ☐ EBOOK ☐ AUDIOBOOK

SOURCE ☐ BOUGHT ☐ BORROWED ☐ GIFTED ☐ OTHER ______

DESCRIBE THE BOOK IN ONE SENTENCE

WHAT DREW ME TO THIS BOOK?

QUOTES/FAVORITE PASSAGES

REVIEW

STARTED BOOK

FINISHED BOOK

WOULD RECOMMEND?
☐ YES ☐ NO ☐ MAYBE

RECOMMEND TO

WOULD READ AGAIN?
☐ YES ☐ NO ☐ MAYBE

WOULD READ OTHER AUTHOR'S BOOKS?
☐ YES ☐ NO ☐ MAYBE

BOOK RATING

EASE OF READING
☆☆☆☆☆

CHARACTERS
☆☆☆☆☆

PLOT
☆☆☆☆☆

ENJOYABILITY
☆☆☆☆☆

OVERALL RATING
☆☆☆☆☆

BOOK REVIEW

#

TITLE	AUTHOR

☐ FICTION
☐ NON-FICTION

GENRE ____

FIRST PUBLISHED ____

NEW-TO-ME AUTHOR?
☐ YES ☐ NO

PAGE COUNT ____

FORMAT ☐ HARDCOVER ☐ PAPERBACK ☐ EBOOK ☐ AUDIOBOOK

SOURCE ☐ BOUGHT ☐ BORROWED ☐ GIFTED ☐ OTHER ____

STARTED BOOK ____

FINISHED BOOK ____

WOULD RECOMMEND?
☐ YES ☐ NO ☐ MAYBE

RECOMMEND TO ____

WOULD READ AGAIN?
☐ YES ☐ NO ☐ MAYBE

WOULD READ OTHER AUTHOR'S BOOKS?
☐ YES ☐ NO ☐ MAYBE

BOOK RATING

EASE OF READING
☆☆☆☆☆

CHARACTERS
☆☆☆☆☆

PLOT
☆☆☆☆☆

ENJOYABILITY
☆☆☆☆☆

OVERALL RATING
☆☆☆☆☆

DESCRIBE THE BOOK IN ONE SENTENCE ____

WHAT DREW ME TO THIS BOOK? ____

QUOTES/FAVORITE PASSAGES ____

REVIEW ____

BOOK REVIEW

#

TITLE	AUTHOR

☐ FICTION
☐ NON-FICTION

GENRE ________

FIRST PUBLISHED ________

NEW-TO-ME AUTHOR?
☐ YES ☐ NO

PAGE COUNT ________

FORMAT ☐ HARDCOVER ☐ PAPERBACK ☐ EBOOK ☐ AUDIOBOOK

SOURCE ☐ BOUGHT ☐ BORROWED ☐ GIFTED ☐ OTHER ________

DESCRIBE THE BOOK IN ONE SENTENCE

____

WHAT DREW ME TO THIS BOOK?

____

QUOTES/FAVORITE PASSAGES

____

____

____

____

____

____

REVIEW

____

____

____

____

____

____

____

____

STARTED BOOK

____

FINISHED BOOK

____

WOULD RECOMMEND?

☐ YES ☐ NO ☐ MAYBE

RECOMMEND TO

____

WOULD READ AGAIN?

☐ YES ☐ NO ☐ MAYBE

WOULD READ OTHER AUTHOR'S BOOKS?

☐ YES ☐ NO ☐ MAYBE

BOOK RATING

EASE OF READING

☆☆☆☆☆

CHARACTERS

☆☆☆☆☆

PLOT

☆☆☆☆☆

ENJOYABILITY

☆☆☆☆☆

OVERALL RATING

☆☆☆☆☆

BOOK REVIEW

#

TITLE	AUTHOR

☐ FICTION
☐ NON-FICTION

GENRE

FIRST PUBLISHED

NEW-TO-ME AUTHOR? ☐ YES ☐ NO

PAGE COUNT

FORMAT ☐ HARDCOVER ☐ PAPERBACK ☐ EBOOK ☐ AUDIOBOOK

SOURCE ☐ BOUGHT ☐ BORROWED ☐ GIFTED ☐ OTHER

STARTED BOOK

FINISHED BOOK

WOULD RECOMMEND?
☐ YES ☐ NO ☐ MAYBE

RECOMMEND TO

WOULD READ AGAIN?
☐ YES ☐ NO ☐ MAYBE

WOULD READ OTHER AUTHOR'S BOOKS?
☐ YES ☐ NO ☐ MAYBE

BOOK RATING

EASE OF READING
☆☆☆☆☆

CHARACTERS
☆☆☆☆☆

PLOT
☆☆☆☆☆

ENJOYABILITY
☆☆☆☆☆

OVERALL RATING
☆☆☆☆☆

DESCRIBE THE BOOK IN ONE SENTENCE

WHAT DREW ME TO THIS BOOK?

QUOTES/FAVORITE PASSAGES

REVIEW

BOOK REVIEW

#

TITLE	AUTHOR

☐ FICTION
☐ NON-FICTION

GENRE ____________

FIRST PUBLISHED ____________

NEW-TO-ME AUTHOR?
☐ YES ☐ NO

PAGE COUNT ________

FORMAT ☐ HARDCOVER ☐ PAPERBACK ☐ EBOOK ☐ AUDIOBOOK

SOURCE ☐ BOUGHT ☐ BORROWED ☐ GIFTED ☐ OTHER ________

DESCRIBE THE BOOK IN ONE SENTENCE

WHAT DREW ME TO THIS BOOK?

QUOTES/FAVORITE PASSAGES

REVIEW

STARTED BOOK

FINISHED BOOK

WOULD RECOMMEND?
☐ YES ☐ NO ☐ MAYBE

RECOMMEND TO

WOULD READ AGAIN?
☐ YES ☐ NO ☐ MAYBE

WOULD READ OTHER AUTHOR'S BOOKS?
☐ YES ☐ NO ☐ MAYBE

BOOK RATING

EASE OF READING
☆☆☆☆☆

CHARACTERS
☆☆☆☆☆

PLOT
☆☆☆☆☆

ENJOYABILITY
☆☆☆☆☆

OVERALL RATING
☆☆☆☆☆

BOOK REVIEW

#

TITLE	AUTHOR

☐ FICTION
☐ NON-FICTION

GENRE ____________

FIRST PUBLISHED ____________

NEW-TO-ME AUTHOR?
☐ YES ☐ NO

PAGE COUNT ________

FORMAT ☐ HARDCOVER ☐ PAPERBACK ☐ EBOOK ☐ AUDIOBOOK

SOURCE ☐ BOUGHT ☐ BORROWED ☐ GIFTED ☐ OTHER ________

STARTED BOOK ____________

FINISHED BOOK ____________

WOULD RECOMMEND?
☐ YES ☐ NO ☐ MAYBE

RECOMMEND TO ____________

WOULD READ AGAIN?
☐ YES ☐ NO ☐ MAYBE

WOULD READ OTHER AUTHOR'S BOOKS?
☐ YES ☐ NO ☐ MAYBE

BOOK RATING

EASE OF READING
☆☆☆☆☆

CHARACTERS
☆☆☆☆☆

PLOT
☆☆☆☆☆

ENJOYABILITY
☆☆☆☆☆

OVERALL RATING
☆☆☆☆☆

DESCRIBE THE BOOK IN ONE SENTENCE ____________

WHAT DREW ME TO THIS BOOK? ____________

QUOTES/FAVORITE PASSAGES ____________

REVIEW ____________

BOOK REVIEW

#

TITLE	AUTHOR

☐ FICTION
☐ NON-FICTION

GENRE

FIRST PUBLISHED

NEW-TO-ME AUTHOR?
☐ YES ☐ NO

PAGE COUNT

FORMAT ☐ HARDCOVER ☐ PAPERBACK ☐ EBOOK ☐ AUDIOBOOK

SOURCE ☐ BOUGHT ☐ BORROWED ☐ GIFTED ☐ OTHER

DESCRIBE THE BOOK IN ONE SENTENCE

WHAT DREW ME TO THIS BOOK?

QUOTES/FAVORITE PASSAGES

REVIEW

STARTED BOOK

FINISHED BOOK

WOULD RECOMMEND?
☐ YES ☐ NO ☐ MAYBE

RECOMMEND TO

WOULD READ AGAIN?
☐ YES ☐ NO ☐ MAYBE

WOULD READ OTHER AUTHOR'S BOOKS?
☐ YES ☐ NO ☐ MAYBE

BOOK RATING

EASE OF READING
☆☆☆☆☆

CHARACTERS
☆☆☆☆☆

PLOT
☆☆☆☆☆

ENJOYABILITY
☆☆☆☆☆

OVERALL RATING
☆☆☆☆☆

BOOK REVIEW

#

TITLE	AUTHOR

☐ FICTION
☐ NON-FICTION

GENRE

FIRST PUBLISHED

NEW-TO-ME AUTHOR? ☐ YES ☐ NO

PAGE COUNT

FORMAT ☐ HARDCOVER ☐ PAPERBACK ☐ EBOOK ☐ AUDIOBOOK

SOURCE ☐ BOUGHT ☐ BORROWED ☐ GIFTED ☐ OTHER

STARTED BOOK

FINISHED BOOK

WOULD RECOMMEND?
☐ YES ☐ NO ☐ MAYBE

RECOMMEND TO

WOULD READ AGAIN?
☐ YES ☐ NO ☐ MAYBE

WOULD READ OTHER AUTHOR'S BOOKS?
☐ YES ☐ NO ☐ MAYBE

BOOK RATING

EASE OF READING
☆☆☆☆☆

CHARACTERS
☆☆☆☆☆

PLOT
☆☆☆☆☆

ENJOYABILITY
☆☆☆☆☆

OVERALL RATING
☆☆☆☆☆

DESCRIBE THE BOOK IN ONE SENTENCE

WHAT DREW ME TO THIS BOOK?

QUOTES/FAVORITE PASSAGES

REVIEW

BOOK REVIEW

#

TITLE	AUTHOR

☐ FICTION
☐ NON-FICTION

GENRE ____________

FIRST PUBLISHED ____________

NEW-TO-ME AUTHOR? ☐ YES ☐ NO

PAGE COUNT ________

FORMAT ☐ HARDCOVER ☐ PAPERBACK ☐ EBOOK ☐ AUDIOBOOK

SOURCE ☐ BOUGHT ☐ BORROWED ☐ GIFTED ☐ OTHER ________

DESCRIBE THE BOOK IN ONE SENTENCE

WHAT DREW ME TO THIS BOOK?

QUOTES/FAVORITE PASSAGES

REVIEW

STARTED BOOK

FINISHED BOOK

WOULD RECOMMEND?

☐ YES ☐ NO ☐ MAYBE

RECOMMEND TO

WOULD READ AGAIN?

☐ YES ☐ NO ☐ MAYBE

WOULD READ OTHER AUTHOR'S BOOKS?

☐ YES ☐ NO ☐ MAYBE

BOOK RATING

EASE OF READING ☆☆☆☆☆

CHARACTERS ☆☆☆☆☆

PLOT ☆☆☆☆☆

ENJOYABILITY ☆☆☆☆☆

OVERALL RATING ☆☆☆☆☆

BOOK REVIEW

#

TITLE	AUTHOR

☐ FICTION ☐ NON-FICTION

GENRE

FIRST PUBLISHED

NEW-TO-ME AUTHOR? ☐ YES ☐ NO

PAGE COUNT

FORMAT ☐ HARDCOVER ☐ PAPERBACK ☐ EBOOK ☐ AUDIOBOOK

SOURCE ☐ BOUGHT ☐ BORROWED ☐ GIFTED ☐ OTHER

STARTED BOOK

FINISHED BOOK

WOULD RECOMMEND?

☐ YES ☐ NO ☐ MAYBE

RECOMMEND TO

WOULD READ AGAIN?

☐ YES ☐ NO ☐ MAYBE

WOULD READ OTHER AUTHOR'S BOOKS?

☐ YES ☐ NO ☐ MAYBE

BOOK RATING

EASE OF READING

☆☆☆☆☆

CHARACTERS

☆☆☆☆☆

PLOT

☆☆☆☆☆

ENJOYABILITY

☆☆☆☆☆

OVERALL RATING

☆☆☆☆☆

DESCRIBE THE BOOK IN ONE SENTENCE

WHAT DREW ME TO THIS BOOK?

QUOTES/FAVORITE PASSAGES

REVIEW

BOOK REVIEW

#

TITLE	AUTHOR

☐ FICTION
☐ NON-FICTION

GENRE

FIRST PUBLISHED

NEW-TO-ME AUTHOR? ☐ YES ☐ NO

PAGE COUNT

FORMAT ☐ HARDCOVER ☐ PAPERBACK ☐ EBOOK ☐ AUDIOBOOK

SOURCE ☐ BOUGHT ☐ BORROWED ☐ GIFTED ☐ OTHER

DESCRIBE THE BOOK IN ONE SENTENCE

WHAT DREW ME TO THIS BOOK?

QUOTES/FAVORITE PASSAGES

REVIEW

STARTED BOOK

FINISHED BOOK

WOULD RECOMMEND?

☐ YES ☐ NO ☐ MAYBE

RECOMMEND TO

WOULD READ AGAIN?

☐ YES ☐ NO ☐ MAYBE

WOULD READ OTHER AUTHOR'S BOOKS?

☐ YES ☐ NO ☐ MAYBE

BOOK RATING

EASE OF READING

☆☆☆☆☆

CHARACTERS

☆☆☆☆☆

PLOT

☆☆☆☆☆

ENJOYABILITY

☆☆☆☆☆

OVERALL RATING

☆☆☆☆☆

BOOK REVIEW

\#

TITLE	AUTHOR

☐ FICTION
☐ NON-FICTION

GENRE ______

FIRST PUBLISHED ______

NEW-TO-ME AUTHOR? ☐ YES ☐ NO

PAGE COUNT ______

FORMAT ☐ HARDCOVER ☐ PAPERBACK ☐ EBOOK ☐ AUDIOBOOK

SOURCE ☐ BOUGHT ☐ BORROWED ☐ GIFTED ☐ OTHER ______

STARTED BOOK ______

FINISHED BOOK ______

WOULD RECOMMEND?
☐ YES ☐ NO ☐ MAYBE

RECOMMEND TO ______

WOULD READ AGAIN?
☐ YES ☐ NO ☐ MAYBE

WOULD READ OTHER AUTHOR'S BOOKS?
☐ YES ☐ NO ☐ MAYBE

BOOK RATING

EASE OF READING ☆☆☆☆☆

CHARACTERS ☆☆☆☆☆

PLOT ☆☆☆☆☆

ENJOYABILITY ☆☆☆☆☆

OVERALL RATING ☆☆☆☆☆

DESCRIBE THE BOOK IN ONE SENTENCE ______

WHAT DREW ME TO THIS BOOK? ______

QUOTES/FAVORITE PASSAGES ______

REVIEW ______

BOOK REVIEW

#

TITLE	AUTHOR

☐ FICTION
☐ NON-FICTION

GENRE ______________

FIRST PUBLISHED ______________

NEW-TO-ME AUTHOR? ☐ YES ☐ NO

PAGE COUNT ________

FORMAT ☐ HARDCOVER ☐ PAPERBACK ☐ EBOOK ☐ AUDIOBOOK

SOURCE ☐ BOUGHT ☐ BORROWED ☐ GIFTED ☐ OTHER ________

DESCRIBE THE BOOK IN ONE SENTENCE

____

WHAT DREW ME TO THIS BOOK?

____

QUOTES/FAVORITE PASSAGES

____

____

____

____

____

____

REVIEW

____

____

____

____

____

____

____

____

STARTED BOOK

____

FINISHED BOOK

____

WOULD RECOMMEND?

☐ YES ☐ NO ☐ MAYBE

RECOMMEND TO

____

WOULD READ AGAIN?

☐ YES ☐ NO ☐ MAYBE

WOULD READ OTHER AUTHOR'S BOOKS?

☐ YES ☐ NO ☐ MAYBE

BOOK RATING

EASE OF READING

☆☆☆☆☆

CHARACTERS

☆☆☆☆☆

PLOT

☆☆☆☆☆

ENJOYABILITY

☆☆☆☆☆

OVERALL RATING

☆☆☆☆☆

BOOK REVIEW

#

TITLE	AUTHOR

☐ FICTION
☐ NON-FICTION

GENRE ____________

FIRST PUBLISHED ____________

NEW-TO-ME AUTHOR?
☐ YES ☐ NO

PAGE COUNT ________

FORMAT ☐ HARDCOVER ☐ PAPERBACK ☐ EBOOK ☐ AUDIOBOOK

SOURCE ☐ BOUGHT ☐ BORROWED ☐ GIFTED ☐ OTHER ________

STARTED BOOK ____________

FINISHED BOOK ____________

WOULD RECOMMEND?
☐ YES ☐ NO ☐ MAYBE

RECOMMEND TO ____________

WOULD READ AGAIN?
☐ YES ☐ NO ☐ MAYBE

WOULD READ OTHER AUTHOR'S BOOKS?
☐ YES ☐ NO ☐ MAYBE

BOOK RATING

EASE OF READING
☆☆☆☆☆

CHARACTERS
☆☆☆☆☆

PLOT
☆☆☆☆☆

ENJOYABILITY
☆☆☆☆☆

OVERALL RATING
☆☆☆☆☆

DESCRIBE THE BOOK IN ONE SENTENCE ____________

WHAT DREW ME TO THIS BOOK? ____________

QUOTES/FAVORITE PASSAGES ____________

REVIEW ____________

BOOK REVIEW

#

TITLE	AUTHOR

☐ FICTION GENRE FIRST PUBLISHED

☐ NON-FICTION

NEW-TO-ME AUTHOR? ☐ YES ☐ NO

PAGE COUNT

FORMAT ☐ HARDCOVER ☐ PAPERBACK ☐ EBOOK ☐ AUDIOBOOK

SOURCE ☐ BOUGHT ☐ BORROWED ☐ GIFTED ☐ OTHER

DESCRIBE THE BOOK IN ONE SENTENCE

WHAT DREW ME TO THIS BOOK?

QUOTES/FAVORITE PASSAGES

REVIEW

STARTED BOOK

FINISHED BOOK

WOULD RECOMMEND?

☐ YES ☐ NO ☐ MAYBE

RECOMMEND TO

WOULD READ AGAIN?

☐ YES ☐ NO ☐ MAYBE

WOULD READ OTHER AUTHOR'S BOOKS?

☐ YES ☐ NO ☐ MAYBE

BOOK RATING

EASE OF READING

☆☆☆☆☆

CHARACTERS

☆☆☆☆☆

PLOT

☆☆☆☆☆

ENJOYABILITY

☆☆☆☆☆

OVERALL RATING

☆☆☆☆☆

BOOK REVIEW

#

- [ ] FICTION
- [ ] NON-FICTION

TITLE	AUTHOR

GENRE

FIRST PUBLISHED

NEW-TO-ME AUTHOR?

☐ YES ☐ NO

PAGE COUNT

FORMAT ☐ HARDCOVER ☐ PAPERBACK ☐ EBOOK ☐ AUDIOBOOK

SOURCE ☐ BOUGHT ☐ BORROWED ☐ GIFTED ☐ OTHER

STARTED BOOK

FINISHED BOOK

WOULD RECOMMEND?

☐ YES ☐ NO ☐ MAYBE

RECOMMEND TO

WOULD READ AGAIN?

☐ YES ☐ NO ☐ MAYBE

WOULD READ OTHER AUTHOR'S BOOKS?

☐ YES ☐ NO ☐ MAYBE

BOOK RATING

EASE OF READING

☆☆☆☆☆

CHARACTERS

☆☆☆☆☆

PLOT

☆☆☆☆☆

ENJOYABILITY

☆☆☆☆☆

OVERALL RATING

☆☆☆☆☆

DESCRIBE THE BOOK IN ONE SENTENCE

WHAT DREW ME TO THIS BOOK?

QUOTES/FAVORITE PASSAGES

REVIEW

BOOK REVIEW

TITLE	AUTHOR

#

☐ FICTION
☐ NON-FICTION

GENRE

FIRST PUBLISHED

NEW-TO-ME AUTHOR?
☐ YES ☐ NO

PAGE COUNT

FORMAT ☐ HARDCOVER ☐ PAPERBACK ☐ EBOOK ☐ AUDIOBOOK

SOURCE ☐ BOUGHT ☐ BORROWED ☐ GIFTED ☐ OTHER

DESCRIBE THE BOOK IN ONE SENTENCE

WHAT DREW ME TO THIS BOOK?

QUOTES/FAVORITE PASSAGES

REVIEW

STARTED BOOK

FINISHED BOOK

WOULD RECOMMEND?
☐ YES ☐ NO ☐ MAYBE

RECOMMEND TO

WOULD READ AGAIN?
☐ YES ☐ NO ☐ MAYBE

WOULD READ OTHER AUTHOR'S BOOKS?
☐ YES ☐ NO ☐ MAYBE

BOOK RATING

EASE OF READING
☆☆☆☆☆

CHARACTERS
☆☆☆☆☆

PLOT
☆☆☆☆☆

ENJOYABILITY
☆☆☆☆☆

OVERALL RATING
☆☆☆☆☆

BOOK REVIEW

#

TITLE	AUTHOR

☐ FICTION
☐ NON-FICTION

GENRE

FIRST PUBLISHED

NEW-TO-ME AUTHOR?
☐ YES ☐ NO

PAGE COUNT

FORMAT ☐ HARDCOVER ☐ PAPERBACK ☐ EBOOK ☐ AUDIOBOOK

SOURCE ☐ BOUGHT ☐ BORROWED ☐ GIFTED ☐ OTHER ______

STARTED BOOK

FINISHED BOOK

WOULD RECOMMEND?
☐ YES ☐ NO ☐ MAYBE

RECOMMEND TO

WOULD READ AGAIN?
☐ YES ☐ NO ☐ MAYBE

WOULD READ OTHER AUTHOR'S BOOKS?
☐ YES ☐ NO ☐ MAYBE

BOOK RATING

EASE OF READING
☆☆☆☆☆

CHARACTERS
☆☆☆☆☆

PLOT
☆☆☆☆☆

ENJOYABILITY
☆☆☆☆☆

OVERALL RATING
☆☆☆☆☆

DESCRIBE THE BOOK IN ONE SENTENCE

WHAT DREW ME TO THIS BOOK?

QUOTES/FAVORITE PASSAGES

REVIEW

BOOK REVIEW

#

TITLE	AUTHOR

☐ FICTION
☐ NON-FICTION

GENRE

FIRST PUBLISHED

NEW-TO-ME AUTHOR?
☐ YES ☐ NO

PAGE COUNT

FORMAT ☐ HARDCOVER ☐ PAPERBACK ☐ EBOOK ☐ AUDIOBOOK

SOURCE ☐ BOUGHT ☐ BORROWED ☐ GIFTED ☐ OTHER

DESCRIBE THE BOOK IN ONE SENTENCE

WHAT DREW ME TO THIS BOOK?

QUOTES/FAVORITE PASSAGES

REVIEW

STARTED BOOK

FINISHED BOOK

WOULD RECOMMEND?
☐ YES ☐ NO ☐ MAYBE

RECOMMEND TO

WOULD READ AGAIN?
☐ YES ☐ NO ☐ MAYBE

WOULD READ OTHER AUTHOR'S BOOKS?
☐ YES ☐ NO ☐ MAYBE

BOOK RATING

EASE OF READING
☆☆☆☆☆

CHARACTERS
☆☆☆☆☆

PLOT
☆☆☆☆☆

ENJOYABILITY
☆☆☆☆☆

OVERALL RATING
☆☆☆☆☆

BOOK REVIEW

#

TITLE	AUTHOR

☐ FICTION
☐ NON-FICTION

GENRE ____________

FIRST PUBLISHED ____________

NEW-TO-ME AUTHOR?
☐ YES ☐ NO

PAGE COUNT ________

FORMAT ☐ HARDCOVER ☐ PAPERBACK ☐ EBOOK ☐ AUDIOBOOK

SOURCE ☐ BOUGHT ☐ BORROWED ☐ GIFTED ☐ OTHER ________

STARTED BOOK

FINISHED BOOK

WOULD RECOMMEND?
☐ YES ☐ NO ☐ MAYBE

RECOMMEND TO

WOULD READ AGAIN?
☐ YES ☐ NO ☐ MAYBE

WOULD READ OTHER AUTHOR'S BOOKS?
☐ YES ☐ NO ☐ MAYBE

BOOK RATING

EASE OF READING
☆☆☆☆☆

CHARACTERS
☆☆☆☆☆

PLOT
☆☆☆☆☆

ENJOYABILITY
☆☆☆☆☆

OVERALL RATING
☆☆☆☆☆

DESCRIBE THE BOOK IN ONE SENTENCE

WHAT DREW ME TO THIS BOOK?

QUOTES/FAVORITE PASSAGES

REVIEW

BOOK REVIEW

#

TITLE	AUTHOR

☐ FICTION
☐ NON-FICTION

GENRE ______

FIRST PUBLISHED ______

NEW-TO-ME AUTHOR? ☐ YES ☐ NO

PAGE COUNT ______

FORMAT ☐ HARDCOVER ☐ PAPERBACK ☐ EBOOK ☐ AUDIOBOOK

SOURCE ☐ BOUGHT ☐ BORROWED ☐ GIFTED ☐ OTHER ______

DESCRIBE THE BOOK IN ONE SENTENCE

______

WHAT DREW ME TO THIS BOOK?

______

QUOTES/FAVORITE PASSAGES

______

______

______

______

______

______

REVIEW

______

______

______

______

______

______

______

______

STARTED BOOK

______

FINISHED BOOK

______

WOULD RECOMMEND?

☐ YES ☐ NO ☐ MAYBE

RECOMMEND TO

______

WOULD READ AGAIN?

☐ YES ☐ NO ☐ MAYBE

WOULD READ OTHER AUTHOR'S BOOKS?

☐ YES ☐ NO ☐ MAYBE

BOOK RATING

EASE OF READING

☆☆☆☆☆

CHARACTERS

☆☆☆☆☆

PLOT

☆☆☆☆☆

ENJOYABILITY

☆☆☆☆☆

OVERALL RATING

☆☆☆☆☆

BOOK REVIEW

#

TITLE	AUTHOR

☐ FICTION ☐ NON-FICTION

GENRE

FIRST PUBLISHED

NEW-TO-ME AUTHOR?
☐ YES ☐ NO

PAGE COUNT

FORMAT ☐ HARDCOVER ☐ PAPERBACK ☐ EBOOK ☐ AUDIOBOOK

SOURCE ☐ BOUGHT ☐ BORROWED ☐ GIFTED ☐ OTHER ______

STARTED BOOK

FINISHED BOOK

WOULD RECOMMEND?
☐ YES ☐ NO ☐ MAYBE

RECOMMEND TO

WOULD READ AGAIN?
☐ YES ☐ NO ☐ MAYBE

WOULD READ OTHER AUTHOR'S BOOKS?
☐ YES ☐ NO ☐ MAYBE

BOOK RATING

EASE OF READING
☆☆☆☆☆

CHARACTERS
☆☆☆☆☆

PLOT
☆☆☆☆☆

ENJOYABILITY
☆☆☆☆☆

OVERALL RATING
☆☆☆☆☆

DESCRIBE THE BOOK IN ONE SENTENCE

WHAT DREW ME TO THIS BOOK?

QUOTES/FAVORITE PASSAGES

REVIEW

BOOK REVIEW

#

TITLE	AUTHOR

☐ FICTION
☐ NON-FICTION

GENRE ______

FIRST PUBLISHED ______

NEW-TO-ME AUTHOR?
☐ YES ☐ NO

PAGE COUNT ______

FORMAT ☐ HARDCOVER ☐ PAPERBACK ☐ EBOOK ☐ AUDIOBOOK

SOURCE ☐ BOUGHT ☐ BORROWED ☐ GIFTED ☐ OTHER ______

DESCRIBE THE BOOK IN ONE SENTENCE

WHAT DREW ME TO THIS BOOK?

QUOTES/FAVORITE PASSAGES

REVIEW

STARTED BOOK

FINISHED BOOK

WOULD RECOMMEND?
☐ YES ☐ NO ☐ MAYBE

RECOMMEND TO

WOULD READ AGAIN?
☐ YES ☐ NO ☐ MAYBE

WOULD READ OTHER AUTHOR'S BOOKS?
☐ YES ☐ NO ☐ MAYBE

BOOK RATING

EASE OF READING
☆☆☆☆☆

CHARACTERS
☆☆☆☆☆

PLOT
☆☆☆☆☆

ENJOYABILITY
☆☆☆☆☆

OVERALL RATING
☆☆☆☆☆

BOOK REVIEW

#

TITLE	AUTHOR

☐ FICTION
☐ NON-FICTION

GENRE ______

FIRST PUBLISHED ______

NEW-TO-ME AUTHOR? ☐ YES ☐ NO

PAGE COUNT ______

FORMAT ☐ HARDCOVER ☐ PAPERBACK ☐ EBOOK ☐ AUDIOBOOK

SOURCE ☐ BOUGHT ☐ BORROWED ☐ GIFTED ☐ OTHER ______

STARTED BOOK ______

FINISHED BOOK ______

WOULD RECOMMEND?
☐ YES ☐ NO ☐ MAYBE

RECOMMEND TO ______

WOULD READ AGAIN?
☐ YES ☐ NO ☐ MAYBE

WOULD READ OTHER AUTHOR'S BOOKS?
☐ YES ☐ NO ☐ MAYBE

BOOK RATING

EASE OF READING ☆☆☆☆☆

CHARACTERS ☆☆☆☆☆

PLOT ☆☆☆☆☆

ENJOYABILITY ☆☆☆☆☆

OVERALL RATING ☆☆☆☆☆

DESCRIBE THE BOOK IN ONE SENTENCE ______

WHAT DREW ME TO THIS BOOK? ______

QUOTES/FAVORITE PASSAGES ______

REVIEW ______

BOOK REVIEW

#

TITLE	AUTHOR

☐ FICTION
☐ NON-FICTION

GENRE ______

FIRST PUBLISHED ______

NEW-TO-ME AUTHOR?
☐ YES ☐ NO

PAGE COUNT ______

FORMAT ☐ HARDCOVER ☐ PAPERBACK ☐ EBOOK ☐ AUDIOBOOK

SOURCE ☐ BOUGHT ☐ BORROWED ☐ GIFTED ☐ OTHER ______

DESCRIBE THE BOOK IN ONE SENTENCE

WHAT DREW ME TO THIS BOOK?

QUOTES/FAVORITE PASSAGES

REVIEW

STARTED BOOK

FINISHED BOOK

WOULD RECOMMEND?
☐ YES ☐ NO ☐ MAYBE

RECOMMEND TO

WOULD READ AGAIN?
☐ YES ☐ NO ☐ MAYBE

WOULD READ OTHER AUTHOR'S BOOKS?
☐ YES ☐ NO ☐ MAYBE

BOOK RATING

EASE OF READING
☆☆☆☆☆

CHARACTERS
☆☆☆☆☆

PLOT
☆☆☆☆☆

ENJOYABILITY
☆☆☆☆☆

OVERALL RATING
☆☆☆☆☆

BOOK REVIEW

#

TITLE	AUTHOR

☐ FICTION
☐ NON-FICTION

GENRE

FIRST PUBLISHED

NEW-TO-ME AUTHOR?
☐ YES ☐ NO

PAGE COUNT

FORMAT ☐ HARDCOVER ☐ PAPERBACK ☐ EBOOK ☐ AUDIOBOOK

SOURCE ☐ BOUGHT ☐ BORROWED ☐ GIFTED ☐ OTHER

STARTED BOOK

FINISHED BOOK

WOULD RECOMMEND?
☐ YES ☐ NO ☐ MAYBE

RECOMMEND TO

WOULD READ AGAIN?
☐ YES ☐ NO ☐ MAYBE

WOULD READ OTHER AUTHOR'S BOOKS?
☐ YES ☐ NO ☐ MAYBE

BOOK RATING

EASE OF READING
☆☆☆☆☆

CHARACTERS
☆☆☆☆☆

PLOT
☆☆☆☆☆

ENJOYABILITY
☆☆☆☆☆

OVERALL RATING
☆☆☆☆☆

DESCRIBE THE BOOK IN ONE SENTENCE

WHAT DREW ME TO THIS BOOK?

QUOTES/FAVORITE PASSAGES

REVIEW

BOOK REVIEW

#

TITLE	AUTHOR

☐ FICTION
☐ NON-FICTION

GENRE ____________

FIRST PUBLISHED ____________

NEW-TO-ME AUTHOR?
☐ YES ☐ NO

PAGE COUNT ________

FORMAT ☐ HARDCOVER ☐ PAPERBACK ☐ EBOOK ☐ AUDIOBOOK

SOURCE ☐ BOUGHT ☐ BORROWED ☐ GIFTED ☐ OTHER ________

DESCRIBE THE BOOK IN ONE SENTENCE

WHAT DREW ME TO THIS BOOK?

QUOTES/FAVORITE PASSAGES

REVIEW

STARTED BOOK

FINISHED BOOK

WOULD RECOMMEND?
☐ YES ☐ NO ☐ MAYBE

RECOMMEND TO

WOULD READ AGAIN?
☐ YES ☐ NO ☐ MAYBE

WOULD READ OTHER AUTHOR'S BOOKS?
☐ YES ☐ NO ☐ MAYBE

BOOK RATING

EASE OF READING
☆☆☆☆☆

CHARACTERS
☆☆☆☆☆

PLOT
☆☆☆☆☆

ENJOYABILITY
☆☆☆☆☆

OVERALL RATING
☆☆☆☆☆

BOOK REVIEW

#

TITLE	AUTHOR

☐ FICTION
☐ NON-FICTION

GENRE

FIRST PUBLISHED

NEW-TO-ME AUTHOR?
☐ YES ☐ NO

PAGE COUNT

FORMAT ☐ HARDCOVER ☐ PAPERBACK ☐ EBOOK ☐ AUDIOBOOK

SOURCE ☐ BOUGHT ☐ BORROWED ☐ GIFTED ☐ OTHER

STARTED BOOK

FINISHED BOOK

WOULD RECOMMEND?
☐ YES ☐ NO ☐ MAYBE

RECOMMEND TO

WOULD READ AGAIN?
☐ YES ☐ NO ☐ MAYBE

WOULD READ OTHER AUTHOR'S BOOKS?
☐ YES ☐ NO ☐ MAYBE

BOOK RATING

EASE OF READING
☆☆☆☆☆

CHARACTERS
☆☆☆☆☆

PLOT
☆☆☆☆☆

ENJOYABILITY
☆☆☆☆☆

OVERALL RATING
☆☆☆☆☆

DESCRIBE THE BOOK IN ONE SENTENCE

WHAT DREW ME TO THIS BOOK?

QUOTES/FAVORITE PASSAGES

REVIEW

BOOK REVIEW

#

TITLE	AUTHOR

☐ FICTION
☐ NON-FICTION

GENRE

FIRST PUBLISHED

NEW-TO-ME AUTHOR?
☐ YES ☐ NO

PAGE COUNT

FORMAT ☐ HARDCOVER ☐ PAPERBACK ☐ EBOOK ☐ AUDIOBOOK

SOURCE ☐ BOUGHT ☐ BORROWED ☐ GIFTED ☐ OTHER

DESCRIBE THE BOOK IN ONE SENTENCE

WHAT DREW ME TO THIS BOOK?

QUOTES/FAVORITE PASSAGES

REVIEW

STARTED BOOK

FINISHED BOOK

WOULD RECOMMEND?
☐ YES ☐ NO ☐ MAYBE

RECOMMEND TO

WOULD READ AGAIN?
☐ YES ☐ NO ☐ MAYBE

WOULD READ OTHER AUTHOR'S BOOKS?
☐ YES ☐ NO ☐ MAYBE

BOOK RATING

EASE OF READING
☆☆☆☆☆

CHARACTERS
☆☆☆☆☆

PLOT
☆☆☆☆☆

ENJOYABILITY
☆☆☆☆☆

OVERALL RATING
☆☆☆☆☆

BOOK REVIEW

#

TITLE	AUTHOR

☐ FICTION
☐ NON-FICTION

GENRE

FIRST PUBLISHED

NEW-TO-ME AUTHOR?
☐ YES ☐ NO

PAGE COUNT

FORMAT ☐ HARDCOVER ☐ PAPERBACK ☐ EBOOK ☐ AUDIOBOOK

SOURCE ☐ BOUGHT ☐ BORROWED ☐ GIFTED ☐ OTHER

STARTED BOOK

FINISHED BOOK

WOULD RECOMMEND?
☐ YES ☐ NO ☐ MAYBE

RECOMMEND TO

WOULD READ AGAIN?
☐ YES ☐ NO ☐ MAYBE

WOULD READ OTHER AUTHOR'S BOOKS?
☐ YES ☐ NO ☐ MAYBE

BOOK RATING

EASE OF READING
☆☆☆☆☆

CHARACTERS
☆☆☆☆☆

PLOT
☆☆☆☆☆

ENJOYABILITY
☆☆☆☆☆

OVERALL RATING
☆☆☆☆☆

DESCRIBE THE BOOK IN ONE SENTENCE

WHAT DREW ME TO THIS BOOK?

QUOTES/FAVORITE PASSAGES

REVIEW

BOOK REVIEW

#

TITLE	AUTHOR

☐ FICTION
☐ NON-FICTION

GENRE

FIRST PUBLISHED

NEW-TO-ME AUTHOR? ☐ YES ☐ NO

PAGE COUNT

FORMAT ☐ HARDCOVER ☐ PAPERBACK ☐ EBOOK ☐ AUDIOBOOK

SOURCE ☐ BOUGHT ☐ BORROWED ☐ GIFTED ☐ OTHER

DESCRIBE THE BOOK IN ONE SENTENCE

WHAT DREW ME TO THIS BOOK?

QUOTES/FAVORITE PASSAGES

REVIEW

STARTED BOOK

FINISHED BOOK

WOULD RECOMMEND?

☐ YES ☐ NO ☐ MAYBE

RECOMMEND TO

WOULD READ AGAIN?

☐ YES ☐ NO ☐ MAYBE

WOULD READ OTHER AUTHOR'S BOOKS?

☐ YES ☐ NO ☐ MAYBE

BOOK RATING

EASE OF READING

☆☆☆☆☆

CHARACTERS

☆☆☆☆☆

PLOT

☆☆☆☆☆

ENJOYABILITY

☆☆☆☆☆

OVERALL RATING

☆☆☆☆☆

BOOK REVIEW

#

TITLE	AUTHOR

☐ FICTION
☐ NON-FICTION

GENRE ____________

FIRST PUBLISHED ____________

NEW-TO-ME AUTHOR? ☐ YES ☐ NO

PAGE COUNT ________

FORMAT ☐ HARDCOVER ☐ PAPERBACK ☐ EBOOK ☐ AUDIOBOOK

SOURCE ☐ BOUGHT ☐ BORROWED ☐ GIFTED ☐ OTHER ________

STARTED BOOK ____________

FINISHED BOOK ____________

WOULD RECOMMEND?

☐ YES ☐ NO ☐ MAYBE

RECOMMEND TO ____________

WOULD READ AGAIN?

☐ YES ☐ NO ☐ MAYBE

WOULD READ OTHER AUTHOR'S BOOKS?

☐ YES ☐ NO ☐ MAYBE

BOOK RATING

EASE OF READING ☆☆☆☆☆

CHARACTERS ☆☆☆☆☆

PLOT ☆☆☆☆☆

ENJOYABILITY ☆☆☆☆☆

OVERALL RATING ☆☆☆☆☆

DESCRIBE THE BOOK IN ONE SENTENCE ____________

WHAT DREW ME TO THIS BOOK? ____________

QUOTES/FAVORITE PASSAGES ____________

REVIEW ____________

BOOK REVIEW

#

TITLE	AUTHOR

☐ FICTION ☐ NON-FICTION

GENRE

FIRST PUBLISHED

NEW-TO-ME AUTHOR? ☐ YES ☐ NO

PAGE COUNT

FORMAT ☐ HARDCOVER ☐ PAPERBACK ☐ EBOOK ☐ AUDIOBOOK

SOURCE ☐ BOUGHT ☐ BORROWED ☐ GIFTED ☐ OTHER

DESCRIBE THE BOOK IN ONE SENTENCE

WHAT DREW ME TO THIS BOOK?

QUOTES/FAVORITE PASSAGES

REVIEW

STARTED BOOK

FINISHED BOOK

WOULD RECOMMEND?

☐ YES ☐ NO ☐ MAYBE

RECOMMEND TO

WOULD READ AGAIN?

☐ YES ☐ NO ☐ MAYBE

WOULD READ OTHER AUTHOR'S BOOKS?

☐ YES ☐ NO ☐ MAYBE

BOOK RATING

EASE OF READING

☆☆☆☆☆

CHARACTERS

☆☆☆☆☆

PLOT

☆☆☆☆☆

ENJOYABILITY

☆☆☆☆☆

OVERALL RATING

☆☆☆☆☆

BOOK REVIEW

#

TITLE	AUTHOR

☐ FICTION GENRE FIRST PUBLISHED

☐ NON-FICTION

NEW-TO-ME AUTHOR?

☐ YES ☐ NO

PAGE COUNT

FORMAT ☐ HARDCOVER ☐ PAPERBACK ☐ EBOOK ☐ AUDIOBOOK

SOURCE ☐ BOUGHT ☐ BORROWED ☐ GIFTED ☐ OTHER

STARTED BOOK

FINISHED BOOK

WOULD RECOMMEND?

☐ YES ☐ NO ☐ MAYBE

RECOMMEND TO

WOULD READ AGAIN?

☐ YES ☐ NO ☐ MAYBE

WOULD READ OTHER AUTHOR'S BOOKS?

☐ YES ☐ NO ☐ MAYBE

BOOK RATING

EASE OF READING

☆☆☆☆☆

CHARACTERS

☆☆☆☆☆

PLOT

☆☆☆☆☆

ENJOYABILITY

☆☆☆☆☆

OVERALL RATING

☆☆☆☆☆

DESCRIBE THE BOOK IN ONE SENTENCE

WHAT DREW ME TO THIS BOOK?

QUOTES/FAVORITE PASSAGES

REVIEW

BOOK REVIEW

#

TITLE	AUTHOR

☐ FICTION
☐ NON-FICTION

GENRE

FIRST PUBLISHED

NEW-TO-ME AUTHOR?

☐ YES ☐ NO

PAGE COUNT

FORMAT ☐ HARDCOVER ☐ PAPERBACK ☐ EBOOK ☐ AUDIOBOOK

SOURCE ☐ BOUGHT ☐ BORROWED ☐ GIFTED ☐ OTHER

DESCRIBE THE BOOK IN ONE SENTENCE

WHAT DREW ME TO THIS BOOK?

QUOTES/FAVORITE PASSAGES

REVIEW

STARTED BOOK

FINISHED BOOK

WOULD RECOMMEND?

☐ YES ☐ NO ☐ MAYBE

RECOMMEND TO

WOULD READ AGAIN?

☐ YES ☐ NO ☐ MAYBE

WOULD READ OTHER AUTHOR'S BOOKS?

☐ YES ☐ NO ☐ MAYBE

BOOK RATING

EASE OF READING

☆☆☆☆☆

CHARACTERS

☆☆☆☆☆

PLOT

☆☆☆☆☆

ENJOYABILITY

☆☆☆☆☆

OVERALL RATING

☆☆☆☆☆

BOOK REVIEW

#

TITLE	AUTHOR

☐ FICTION
☐ NON-FICTION

GENRE ____________

FIRST PUBLISHED ____________

NEW-TO-ME AUTHOR?
☐ YES ☐ NO

PAGE COUNT ____________

FORMAT ☐ HARDCOVER ☐ PAPERBACK ☐ EBOOK ☐ AUDIOBOOK

SOURCE ☐ BOUGHT ☐ BORROWED ☐ GIFTED ☐ OTHER ____________

STARTED BOOK ____________

FINISHED BOOK ____________

WOULD RECOMMEND?
☐ YES ☐ NO ☐ MAYBE

RECOMMEND TO ____________

WOULD READ AGAIN?
☐ YES ☐ NO ☐ MAYBE

WOULD READ OTHER AUTHOR'S BOOKS?
☐ YES ☐ NO ☐ MAYBE

BOOK RATING

EASE OF READING
☆☆☆☆☆

CHARACTERS
☆☆☆☆☆

PLOT
☆☆☆☆☆

ENJOYABILITY
☆☆☆☆☆

OVERALL RATING
☆☆☆☆☆

DESCRIBE THE BOOK IN ONE SENTENCE ____________

WHAT DREW ME TO THIS BOOK? ____________

QUOTES/FAVORITE PASSAGES ____________

REVIEW ____________

BOOK REVIEW

#

TITLE	AUTHOR

☐ FICTION
☐ NON-FICTION

GENRE

FIRST PUBLISHED

NEW-TO-ME AUTHOR?
☐ YES ☐ NO

PAGE COUNT

FORMAT ☐ HARDCOVER ☐ PAPERBACK ☐ EBOOK ☐ AUDIOBOOK

SOURCE ☐ BOUGHT ☐ BORROWED ☐ GIFTED ☐ OTHER

DESCRIBE THE BOOK IN ONE SENTENCE

WHAT DREW ME TO THIS BOOK?

QUOTES/FAVORITE PASSAGES

REVIEW

STARTED BOOK

FINISHED BOOK

WOULD RECOMMEND?
☐ YES ☐ NO ☐ MAYBE

RECOMMEND TO

WOULD READ AGAIN?
☐ YES ☐ NO ☐ MAYBE

WOULD READ OTHER AUTHOR'S BOOKS?
☐ YES ☐ NO ☐ MAYBE

BOOK RATING

EASE OF READING
☆☆☆☆☆

CHARACTERS
☆☆☆☆☆

PLOT
☆☆☆☆☆

ENJOYABILITY
☆☆☆☆☆

OVERALL RATING
☆☆☆☆☆

BOOK REVIEW

#

TITLE | AUTHOR

☐ FICTION ☐ NON-FICTION

GENRE

FIRST PUBLISHED

NEW-TO-ME AUTHOR? ☐ YES ☐ NO

PAGE COUNT

FORMAT ☐ HARDCOVER ☐ PAPERBACK ☐ EBOOK ☐ AUDIOBOOK

SOURCE ☐ BOUGHT ☐ BORROWED ☐ GIFTED ☐ OTHER

STARTED BOOK

FINISHED BOOK

WOULD RECOMMEND?

☐ YES ☐ NO ☐ MAYBE

RECOMMEND TO

WOULD READ AGAIN?

☐ YES ☐ NO ☐ MAYBE

WOULD READ OTHER AUTHOR'S BOOKS?

☐ YES ☐ NO ☐ MAYBE

BOOK RATING

EASE OF READING

☆☆☆☆☆

CHARACTERS

☆☆☆☆☆

PLOT

☆☆☆☆☆

ENJOYABILITY

☆☆☆☆☆

OVERALL RATING

☆☆☆☆☆

DESCRIBE THE BOOK IN ONE SENTENCE

WHAT DREW ME TO THIS BOOK?

QUOTES/FAVORITE PASSAGES

REVIEW

BOOK REVIEW

#

TITLE	AUTHOR

☐ FICTION
☐ NON-FICTION

GENRE ________

FIRST PUBLISHED ________

NEW-TO-ME AUTHOR?
☐ YES ☐ NO

PAGE COUNT ________

FORMAT ☐ HARDCOVER ☐ PAPERBACK ☐ EBOOK ☐ AUDIOBOOK

SOURCE ☐ BOUGHT ☐ BORROWED ☐ GIFTED ☐ OTHER ________

DESCRIBE THE BOOK IN ONE SENTENCE

WHAT DREW ME TO THIS BOOK?

QUOTES/FAVORITE PASSAGES

REVIEW

STARTED BOOK

FINISHED BOOK

WOULD RECOMMEND?
☐ YES ☐ NO ☐ MAYBE

RECOMMEND TO

WOULD READ AGAIN?
☐ YES ☐ NO ☐ MAYBE

WOULD READ OTHER AUTHOR'S BOOKS?
☐ YES ☐ NO ☐ MAYBE

BOOK RATING

EASE OF READING
☆☆☆☆☆

CHARACTERS
☆☆☆☆☆

PLOT
☆☆☆☆☆

ENJOYABILITY
☆☆☆☆☆

OVERALL RATING
☆☆☆☆☆

BOOK REVIEW

\#

TITLE	AUTHOR

☐ FICTION
☐ NON-FICTION

GENRE ____

FIRST PUBLISHED ____

NEW-TO-ME AUTHOR? ☐ YES ☐ NO

PAGE COUNT ____

FORMAT ☐ HARDCOVER ☐ PAPERBACK ☐ EBOOK ☐ AUDIOBOOK

SOURCE ☐ BOUGHT ☐ BORROWED ☐ GIFTED ☐ OTHER ____

STARTED BOOK ____

FINISHED BOOK ____

WOULD RECOMMEND?
☐ YES ☐ NO ☐ MAYBE

RECOMMEND TO ____

WOULD READ AGAIN?
☐ YES ☐ NO ☐ MAYBE

WOULD READ OTHER AUTHOR'S BOOKS?
☐ YES ☐ NO ☐ MAYBE

BOOK RATING

EASE OF READING
☆☆☆☆☆

CHARACTERS
☆☆☆☆☆

PLOT
☆☆☆☆☆

ENJOYABILITY
☆☆☆☆☆

OVERALL RATING
☆☆☆☆☆

DESCRIBE THE BOOK IN ONE SENTENCE ____

WHAT DREW ME TO THIS BOOK? ____

QUOTES/FAVORITE PASSAGES ____

REVIEW ____

BOOK REVIEW

#

TITLE	AUTHOR

☐ FICTION
☐ NON-FICTION

GENRE

FIRST PUBLISHED

NEW-TO-ME AUTHOR?
☐ YES ☐ NO

PAGE COUNT

FORMAT ☐ HARDCOVER ☐ PAPERBACK ☐ EBOOK ☐ AUDIOBOOK

SOURCE ☐ BOUGHT ☐ BORROWED ☐ GIFTED ☐ OTHER

DESCRIBE THE BOOK IN ONE SENTENCE

WHAT DREW ME TO THIS BOOK?

QUOTES/FAVORITE PASSAGES

REVIEW

STARTED BOOK

FINISHED BOOK

WOULD RECOMMEND?
☐ YES ☐ NO ☐ MAYBE

RECOMMEND TO

WOULD READ AGAIN?
☐ YES ☐ NO ☐ MAYBE

WOULD READ OTHER AUTHOR'S BOOKS?
☐ YES ☐ NO ☐ MAYBE

BOOK RATING

EASE OF READING
☆☆☆☆☆

CHARACTERS
☆☆☆☆☆

PLOT
☆☆☆☆☆

ENJOYABILITY
☆☆☆☆☆

OVERALL RATING
☆☆☆☆☆

BOOK REVIEW

#

TITLE	AUTHOR

☐ FICTION
☐ NON-FICTION

GENRE

FIRST PUBLISHED

NEW-TO-ME AUTHOR?
☐ YES ☐ NO

PAGE COUNT

FORMAT ☐ HARDCOVER ☐ PAPERBACK ☐ EBOOK ☐ AUDIOBOOK

SOURCE ☐ BOUGHT ☐ BORROWED ☐ GIFTED ☐ OTHER

STARTED BOOK

FINISHED BOOK

WOULD RECOMMEND?
☐ YES ☐ NO ☐ MAYBE

RECOMMEND TO

WOULD READ AGAIN?
☐ YES ☐ NO ☐ MAYBE

WOULD READ OTHER AUTHOR'S BOOKS?
☐ YES ☐ NO ☐ MAYBE

BOOK RATING

EASE OF READING
☆☆☆☆☆

CHARACTERS
☆☆☆☆☆

PLOT
☆☆☆☆☆

ENJOYABILITY
☆☆☆☆☆

OVERALL RATING
☆☆☆☆☆

DESCRIBE THE BOOK IN ONE SENTENCE

WHAT DREW ME TO THIS BOOK?

QUOTES/FAVORITE PASSAGES

REVIEW

BOOK REVIEW

#

TITLE	AUTHOR

☐ FICTION
☐ NON-FICTION

GENRE ____

FIRST PUBLISHED ____

NEW-TO-ME AUTHOR? ☐ YES ☐ NO

PAGE COUNT ____

FORMAT ☐ HARDCOVER ☐ PAPERBACK ☐ EBOOK ☐ AUDIOBOOK

SOURCE ☐ BOUGHT ☐ BORROWED ☐ GIFTED ☐ OTHER ____

DESCRIBE THE BOOK IN ONE SENTENCE

WHAT DREW ME TO THIS BOOK?

QUOTES/FAVORITE PASSAGES

REVIEW

STARTED BOOK

FINISHED BOOK

WOULD RECOMMEND?

☐ YES ☐ NO ☐ MAYBE

RECOMMEND TO

WOULD READ AGAIN?

☐ YES ☐ NO ☐ MAYBE

WOULD READ OTHER AUTHOR'S BOOKS?

☐ YES ☐ NO ☐ MAYBE

BOOK RATING

EASE OF READING ☆☆☆☆☆

CHARACTERS ☆☆☆☆☆

PLOT ☆☆☆☆☆

ENJOYABILITY ☆☆☆☆☆

OVERALL RATING ☆☆☆☆☆

SERIES REVIEWS

SERIES REVIEWS

SERIES REVIEW

#

TITLE	AUTHOR

☐ FICTION
☐ NON-FICTION

GENRE ______

PUBLICATION DATES ______

BOOKS IN SERIES ______

SERIES COMPLETE? ☐ YES ☐ NO

FORMAT ☐ HARDCOVER ☐ PAPERBACK ☐ EBOOK ☐ AUDIOBOOK

SOURCE ☐ BOUGHT ☐ BORROWED ☐ GIFTED ☐ OTHER ______

STARTED SERIES ______

FINISHED SERIES ______

WOULD RECOMMEND?

☐ YES ☐ NO ☐ MAYBE

RECOMMEND TO ______

WOULD READ AGAIN?

☐ YES ☐ NO ☐ MAYBE

WOULD READ OTHER AUTHOR'S BOOKS?

☐ YES ☐ NO ☐ MAYBE

SERIES RATING

EASE OF READING ☆☆☆☆☆

CHARACTERS ☆☆☆☆☆

PLOT ☆☆☆☆☆

ENJOYABILITY ☆☆☆☆☆

OVERALL RATING ☆☆☆☆☆

DESCRIBE THE SERIES IN ONE SENTENCE ______

WHAT DREW ME TO THIS SERIES? ______

QUOTES/FAVORITE PASSAGES ______

REVIEW ______

SERIES REVIEW

#	TITLE	AUTHOR

☐ FICTION
☐ NON-FICTION

GENRE ________

FIRST PUBLISHED ________

BOOKS IN SERIES ________

SERIES COMPLETE? ☐ YES ☐ NO

FORMAT ☐ HARDCOVER ☐ PAPERBACK ☐ EBOOK ☐ AUDIOBOOK

SOURCE ☐ BOUGHT ☐ BORROWED ☐ GIFTED ☐ OTHER ________

DESCRIBE THE SERIES IN ONE SENTENCE

____

WHAT DREW ME TO THIS SERIES?

____

QUOTES/FAVORITE PASSAGES

____

REVIEW

____

STARTED SERIES ________

FINISHED SERIES ________

WOULD RECOMMEND?
☐ YES ☐ NO ☐ MAYBE

RECOMMEND TO ________

WOULD READ AGAIN?
☐ YES ☐ NO ☐ MAYBE

WOULD READ OTHER AUTHOR'S WORKS?
☐ YES ☐ NO ☐ MAYBE

SERIES RATING

EASE OF READING ☆☆☆☆☆

CHARACTERS ☆☆☆☆☆

PLOT ☆☆☆☆☆

ENJOYABILITY ☆☆☆☆☆

OVERALL RATING ☆☆☆☆☆

SERIES REVIEW

#

TITLE	AUTHOR

☐ FICTION
☐ NON-FICTION

GENRE ______

PUBLICATION DATES ______

BOOKS IN SERIES ______

SERIES COMPLETE? ☐ YES ☐ NO

FORMAT ☐ HARDCOVER ☐ PAPERBACK ☐ EBOOK ☐ AUDIOBOOK

SOURCE ☐ BOUGHT ☐ BORROWED ☐ GIFTED ☐ OTHER ______

STARTED SERIES ______

FINISHED SERIES ______

WOULD RECOMMEND?
☐ YES ☐ NO ☐ MAYBE

RECOMMEND TO ______

WOULD READ AGAIN?
☐ YES ☐ NO ☐ MAYBE

WOULD READ OTHER AUTHOR'S BOOKS?
☐ YES ☐ NO ☐ MAYBE

SERIES RATING

EASE OF READING
☆☆☆☆☆

CHARACTERS
☆☆☆☆☆

PLOT
☆☆☆☆☆

ENJOYABILITY
☆☆☆☆☆

OVERALL RATING
☆☆☆☆☆

DESCRIBE THE SERIES IN ONE SENTENCE ______

WHAT DREW ME TO THIS SERIES? ______

QUOTES/FAVORITE PASSAGES ______

REVIEW ______

SERIES REVIEW

#

TITLE	AUTHOR

☐ FICTION
☐ NON-FICTION

GENRE ____________

FIRST PUBLISHED ____________

BOOKS IN SERIES ____________

SERIES COMPLETE? ☐ YES ☐ NO

FORMAT ☐ HARDCOVER ☐ PAPERBACK ☐ EBOOK ☐ AUDIOBOOK

SOURCE ☐ BOUGHT ☐ BORROWED ☐ GIFTED ☐ OTHER ____________

DESCRIBE THE SERIES IN ONE SENTENCE

WHAT DREW ME TO THIS SERIES?

QUOTES/FAVORITE PASSAGES

REVIEW

STARTED SERIES

FINISHED SERIES

WOULD RECOMMEND?
☐ YES ☐ NO ☐ MAYBE

RECOMMEND TO

WOULD READ AGAIN?
☐ YES ☐ NO ☐ MAYBE

WOULD READ OTHER AUTHOR'S WORKS?
☐ YES ☐ NO ☐ MAYBE

SERIES RATING

EASE OF READING
☆☆☆☆☆

CHARACTERS
☆☆☆☆☆

PLOT
☆☆☆☆☆

ENJOYABILITY
☆☆☆☆☆

OVERALL RATING
☆☆☆☆☆

SERIES REVIEW

#

TITLE	AUTHOR

☐ FICTION
☐ NON-FICTION

GENRE

PUBLICATION DATES

BOOKS IN SERIES

SERIES COMPLETE?
☐ YES ☐ NO

FORMAT ☐ HARDCOVER ☐ PAPERBACK ☐ EBOOK ☐ AUDIOBOOK

SOURCE ☐ BOUGHT ☐ BORROWED ☐ GIFTED ☐ OTHER ______

STARTED SERIES

FINISHED SERIES

WOULD RECOMMEND?
☐ YES ☐ NO ☐ MAYBE

RECOMMEND TO

WOULD READ AGAIN?
☐ YES ☐ NO ☐ MAYBE

WOULD READ OTHER AUTHOR'S BOOKS?
☐ YES ☐ NO ☐ MAYBE

SERIES RATING

EASE OF READING
☆☆☆☆☆

CHARACTERS
☆☆☆☆☆

PLOT
☆☆☆☆☆

ENJOYABILITY
☆☆☆☆☆

OVERALL RATING
☆☆☆☆☆

DESCRIBE THE SERIES IN ONE SENTENCE

WHAT DREW ME TO THIS SERIES?

QUOTES/FAVORITE PASSAGES

REVIEW

SERIES REVIEW

TITLE	AUTHOR

#

☐ FICTION
☐ NON-FICTION

GENRE

FIRST PUBLISHED

BOOKS IN SERIES

SERIES COMPLETE? ☐ YES ☐ NO

FORMAT ☐ HARDCOVER ☐ PAPERBACK ☐ EBOOK ☐ AUDIOBOOK

SOURCE ☐ BOUGHT ☐ BORROWED ☐ GIFTED ☐ OTHER ______

DESCRIBE THE SERIES IN ONE SENTENCE

WHAT DREW ME TO THIS SERIES?

QUOTES/FAVORITE PASSAGES

REVIEW

STARTED SERIES

FINISHED SERIES

WOULD RECOMMEND?

☐ YES ☐ NO ☐ MAYBE

RECOMMEND TO

WOULD READ AGAIN?

☐ YES ☐ NO ☐ MAYBE

WOULD READ OTHER AUTHOR'S WORKS?

☐ YES ☐ NO ☐ MAYBE

SERIES RATING

EASE OF READING

☆☆☆☆☆

CHARACTERS

☆☆☆☆☆

PLOT

☆☆☆☆☆

ENJOYABILITY

☆☆☆☆☆

OVERALL RATING

☆☆☆☆☆

SERIES REVIEW

#

TITLE | AUTHOR

☐ FICTION
☐ NON-FICTION

GENRE

PUBLICATION DATES

BOOKS IN SERIES

SERIES COMPLETE?
☐ YES ☐ NO

FORMAT ☐ HARDCOVER ☐ PAPERBACK ☐ EBOOK ☐ AUDIOBOOK

SOURCE ☐ BOUGHT ☐ BORROWED ☐ GIFTED ☐ OTHER

STARTED SERIES

FINISHED SERIES

WOULD RECOMMEND?
☐ YES ☐ NO ☐ MAYBE

RECOMMEND TO

WOULD READ AGAIN?
☐ YES ☐ NO ☐ MAYBE

WOULD READ OTHER AUTHOR'S BOOKS?
☐ YES ☐ NO ☐ MAYBE

SERIES RATING

EASE OF READING
☆☆☆☆☆

CHARACTERS
☆☆☆☆☆

PLOT
☆☆☆☆☆

ENJOYABILITY
☆☆☆☆☆

OVERALL RATING
☆☆☆☆☆

DESCRIBE THE SERIES IN ONE SENTENCE

WHAT DREW ME TO THIS SERIES?

QUOTES/FAVORITE PASSAGES

REVIEW

SERIES REVIEW

#

TITLE	AUTHOR

☐ FICTION
☐ NON-FICTION

GENRE

FIRST PUBLISHED

BOOKS IN SERIES

SERIES COMPLETE?
☐ YES ☐ NO

FORMAT ☐ HARDCOVER ☐ PAPERBACK ☐ EBOOK ☐ AUDIOBOOK

SOURCE ☐ BOUGHT ☐ BORROWED ☐ GIFTED ☐ OTHER

DESCRIBE THE SERIES IN ONE SENTENCE

WHAT DREW ME TO THIS SERIES?

QUOTES/FAVORITE PASSAGES

REVIEW

STARTED SERIES

FINISHED SERIES

WOULD RECOMMEND?
☐ YES ☐ NO ☐ MAYBE

RECOMMEND TO

WOULD READ AGAIN?
☐ YES ☐ NO ☐ MAYBE

WOULD READ OTHER AUTHOR'S WORKS?
☐ YES ☐ NO ☐ MAYBE

SERIES RATING

EASE OF READING
☆☆☆☆☆

CHARACTERS
☆☆☆☆☆

PLOT
☆☆☆☆☆

ENJOYABILITY
☆☆☆☆☆

OVERALL RATING
☆☆☆☆☆

SERIES REVIEW

#

TITLE	AUTHOR

☐ FICTION
☐ NON-FICTION

GENRE

PUBLICATION DATES

BOOKS IN SERIES

SERIES COMPLETE? ☐ YES ☐ NO

FORMAT ☐ HARDCOVER ☐ PAPERBACK ☐ EBOOK ☐ AUDIOBOOK

SOURCE ☐ BOUGHT ☐ BORROWED ☐ GIFTED ☐ OTHER

STARTED SERIES

FINISHED SERIES

WOULD RECOMMEND?

☐ YES ☐ NO ☐ MAYBE

RECOMMEND TO

WOULD READ AGAIN?

☐ YES ☐ NO ☐ MAYBE

WOULD READ OTHER AUTHOR'S BOOKS?

☐ YES ☐ NO ☐ MAYBE

SERIES RATING

EASE OF READING

☆☆☆☆☆

CHARACTERS

☆☆☆☆☆

PLOT

☆☆☆☆☆

ENJOYABILITY

☆☆☆☆☆

OVERALL RATING

☆☆☆☆☆

DESCRIBE THE SERIES IN ONE SENTENCE

WHAT DREW ME TO THIS SERIES?

QUOTES/FAVORITE PASSAGES

REVIEW

SERIES REVIEW

#

TITLE	AUTHOR

☐ FICTION
☐ NON-FICTION

GENRE

FIRST PUBLISHED

BOOKS IN SERIES

SERIES COMPLETE? ☐ YES ☐ NO

FORMAT ☐ HARDCOVER ☐ PAPERBACK ☐ EBOOK ☐ AUDIOBOOK

SOURCE ☐ BOUGHT ☐ BORROWED ☐ GIFTED ☐ OTHER

DESCRIBE THE SERIES IN ONE SENTENCE

WHAT DREW ME TO THIS SERIES?

QUOTES/FAVORITE PASSAGES

REVIEW

STARTED SERIES

FINISHED SERIES

WOULD RECOMMEND?

☐ YES ☐ NO ☐ MAYBE

RECOMMEND TO

WOULD READ AGAIN?

☐ YES ☐ NO ☐ MAYBE

WOULD READ OTHER AUTHOR'S WORKS?

☐ YES ☐ NO ☐ MAYBE

SERIES RATING

EASE OF READING

☆☆☆☆☆

CHARACTERS

☆☆☆☆☆

PLOT

☆☆☆☆☆

ENJOYABILITY

☆☆☆☆☆

OVERALL RATING

☆☆☆☆☆

SERIES REVIEW

#

TITLE	AUTHOR

☐ FICTION
☐ NON-FICTION

GENRE

PUBLICATION DATES

BOOKS IN SERIES

SERIES COMPLETE? ☐ YES ☐ NO

FORMAT ☐ HARDCOVER ☐ PAPERBACK ☐ EBOOK ☐ AUDIOBOOK

SOURCE ☐ BOUGHT ☐ BORROWED ☐ GIFTED ☐ OTHER

STARTED SERIES

FINISHED SERIES

WOULD RECOMMEND?

☐ YES ☐ NO ☐ MAYBE

RECOMMEND TO

WOULD READ AGAIN?

☐ YES ☐ NO ☐ MAYBE

WOULD READ OTHER AUTHOR'S BOOKS?

☐ YES ☐ NO ☐ MAYBE

SERIES RATING

EASE OF READING

☆☆☆☆☆

CHARACTERS

☆☆☆☆☆

PLOT

☆☆☆☆☆

ENJOYABILITY

☆☆☆☆☆

OVERALL RATING

☆☆☆☆☆

DESCRIBE THE SERIES IN ONE SENTENCE

WHAT DREW ME TO THIS SERIES?

QUOTES/FAVORITE PASSAGES

REVIEW

SERIES REVIEW

#

- [ ] FICTION
- [ ] NON-FICTION

TITLE	AUTHOR

GENRE ______

FIRST PUBLISHED ______

BOOKS IN SERIES ______

SERIES COMPLETE? ☐ YES ☐ NO

FORMAT ☐ HARDCOVER ☐ PAPERBACK ☐ EBOOK ☐ AUDIOBOOK

SOURCE ☐ BOUGHT ☐ BORROWED ☐ GIFTED ☐ OTHER ______

DESCRIBE THE SERIES IN ONE SENTENCE

WHAT DREW ME TO THIS SERIES?

QUOTES/FAVORITE PASSAGES

REVIEW

STARTED SERIES

FINISHED SERIES

WOULD RECOMMEND?

☐ YES ☐ NO ☐ MAYBE

RECOMMEND TO

WOULD READ AGAIN?

☐ YES ☐ NO ☐ MAYBE

WOULD READ OTHER AUTHOR'S WORKS?

☐ YES ☐ NO ☐ MAYBE

SERIES RATING

EASE OF READING

☆☆☆☆☆

CHARACTERS

☆☆☆☆☆

PLOT

☆☆☆☆☆

ENJOYABILITY

☆☆☆☆☆

OVERALL RATING

☆☆☆☆☆

SERIES REVIEW

#

TITLE	AUTHOR

☐ FICTION
☐ NON-FICTION

GENRE

PUBLICATION DATES

BOOKS IN SERIES

SERIES COMPLETE?
☐ YES ☐ NO

FORMAT ☐ HARDCOVER ☐ PAPERBACK ☐ EBOOK ☐ AUDIOBOOK

SOURCE ☐ BOUGHT ☐ BORROWED ☐ GIFTED ☐ OTHER

STARTED SERIES

FINISHED SERIES

WOULD RECOMMEND?
☐ YES ☐ NO ☐ MAYBE

RECOMMEND TO

WOULD READ AGAIN?
☐ YES ☐ NO ☐ MAYBE

WOULD READ OTHER AUTHOR'S BOOKS?
☐ YES ☐ NO ☐ MAYBE

SERIES RATING

EASE OF READING
☆☆☆☆☆

CHARACTERS
☆☆☆☆☆

PLOT
☆☆☆☆☆

ENJOYABILITY
☆☆☆☆☆

OVERALL RATING
☆☆☆☆☆

DESCRIBE THE SERIES IN ONE SENTENCE

WHAT DREW ME TO THIS SERIES?

QUOTES/FAVORITE PASSAGES

REVIEW

SERIES REVIEW

#

TITLE	AUTHOR

☐ FICTION
☐ NON-FICTION

GENRE

FIRST PUBLISHED

BOOKS IN SERIES

SERIES COMPLETE?
☐ YES ☐ NO

FORMAT ☐ HARDCOVER ☐ PAPERBACK ☐ EBOOK ☐ AUDIOBOOK

SOURCE ☐ BOUGHT ☐ BORROWED ☐ GIFTED ☐ OTHER

DESCRIBE THE SERIES IN ONE SENTENCE

WHAT DREW ME TO THIS SERIES?

QUOTES/FAVORITE PASSAGES

REVIEW

STARTED SERIES

FINISHED SERIES

WOULD RECOMMEND?
☐ YES ☐ NO ☐ MAYBE

RECOMMEND TO

WOULD READ AGAIN?
☐ YES ☐ NO ☐ MAYBE

WOULD READ OTHER AUTHOR'S WORKS?
☐ YES ☐ NO ☐ MAYBE

SERIES RATING

EASE OF READING
☆☆☆☆☆

CHARACTERS
☆☆☆☆☆

PLOT
☆☆☆☆☆

ENJOYABILITY
☆☆☆☆☆

OVERALL RATING
☆☆☆☆☆

SERIES REVIEW

#

TITLE	AUTHOR

☐ FICTION
☐ NON-FICTION

GENRE ____________

PUBLICATION DATES ____________

BOOKS IN SERIES ____________

SERIES COMPLETE? ☐ YES ☐ NO

FORMAT ☐ HARDCOVER ☐ PAPERBACK ☐ EBOOK ☐ AUDIOBOOK

SOURCE ☐ BOUGHT ☐ BORROWED ☐ GIFTED ☐ OTHER ________

STARTED SERIES ____________

FINISHED SERIES ____________

WOULD RECOMMEND?
☐ YES ☐ NO ☐ MAYBE

RECOMMEND TO ____________

WOULD READ AGAIN?
☐ YES ☐ NO ☐ MAYBE

WOULD READ OTHER AUTHOR'S BOOKS?
☐ YES ☐ NO ☐ MAYBE

SERIES RATING

EASE OF READING
☆☆☆☆☆

CHARACTERS
☆☆☆☆☆

PLOT
☆☆☆☆☆

ENJOYABILITY
☆☆☆☆☆

OVERALL RATING
☆☆☆☆☆

DESCRIBE THE SERIES IN ONE SENTENCE

WHAT DREW ME TO THIS SERIES?

QUOTES/FAVORITE PASSAGES

REVIEW

SERIES REVIEW

#

TITLE	AUTHOR

☐ FICTION
☐ NON-FICTION

GENRE

FIRST PUBLISHED

BOOKS IN SERIES

SERIES COMPLETE? ☐ YES ☐ NO

FORMAT ☐ HARDCOVER ☐ PAPERBACK ☐ EBOOK ☐ AUDIOBOOK

SOURCE ☐ BOUGHT ☐ BORROWED ☐ GIFTED ☐ OTHER

DESCRIBE THE SERIES IN ONE SENTENCE

WHAT DREW ME TO THIS SERIES?

QUOTES/FAVORITE PASSAGES

REVIEW

STARTED SERIES

FINISHED SERIES

WOULD RECOMMEND?

☐ YES ☐ NO ☐ MAYBE

RECOMMEND TO

WOULD READ AGAIN?

☐ YES ☐ NO ☐ MAYBE

WOULD READ OTHER AUTHOR'S WORKS?

☐ YES ☐ NO ☐ MAYBE

SERIES RATING

EASE OF READING

☆☆☆☆☆

CHARACTERS

☆☆☆☆☆

PLOT

☆☆☆☆☆

ENJOYABILITY

☆☆☆☆☆

OVERALL RATING

☆☆☆☆☆

SERIES REVIEW

#

TITLE	AUTHOR

☐ FICTION
☐ NON-FICTION

GENRE

PUBLICATION DATES

BOOKS IN SERIES

SERIES COMPLETE? ☐ YES ☐ NO

FORMAT ☐ HARDCOVER ☐ PAPERBACK ☐ EBOOK ☐ AUDIOBOOK

SOURCE ☐ BOUGHT ☐ BORROWED ☐ GIFTED ☐ OTHER

STARTED SERIES

FINISHED SERIES

WOULD RECOMMEND?

☐ YES ☐ NO ☐ MAYBE

RECOMMEND TO

WOULD READ AGAIN?

☐ YES ☐ NO ☐ MAYBE

WOULD READ OTHER AUTHOR'S BOOKS?

☐ YES ☐ NO ☐ MAYBE

SERIES RATING

EASE OF READING

☆☆☆☆☆

CHARACTERS

☆☆☆☆☆

PLOT

☆☆☆☆☆

ENJOYABILITY

☆☆☆☆☆

OVERALL RATING

☆☆☆☆☆

DESCRIBE THE SERIES IN ONE SENTENCE

WHAT DREW ME TO THIS SERIES?

QUOTES/FAVORITE PASSAGES

REVIEW

SERIES REVIEW

#

TITLE	AUTHOR

☐ FICTION
☐ NON-FICTION

GENRE ____________

FIRST PUBLISHED ____________

BOOKS IN SERIES ____________

SERIES COMPLETE? ☐ YES ☐ NO

FORMAT ☐ HARDCOVER ☐ PAPERBACK ☐ EBOOK ☐ AUDIOBOOK

SOURCE ☐ BOUGHT ☐ BORROWED ☐ GIFTED ☐ OTHER ______

DESCRIBE THE SERIES IN ONE SENTENCE

WHAT DREW ME TO THIS SERIES?

QUOTES/FAVORITE PASSAGES

REVIEW

STARTED SERIES

FINISHED SERIES

WOULD RECOMMEND?
☐ YES ☐ NO ☐ MAYBE

RECOMMEND TO

WOULD READ AGAIN?
☐ YES ☐ NO ☐ MAYBE

WOULD READ OTHER AUTHOR'S WORKS?
☐ YES ☐ NO ☐ MAYBE

SERIES RATING

EASE OF READING
☆☆☆☆☆

CHARACTERS
☆☆☆☆☆

PLOT
☆☆☆☆☆

ENJOYABILITY
☆☆☆☆☆

OVERALL RATING
☆☆☆☆☆

SERIES REVIEW

#

TITLE	AUTHOR

☐ FICTION
☐ NON-FICTION

GENRE ______

PUBLICATION DATES ______

BOOKS IN SERIES ______

SERIES COMPLETE? ☐ YES ☐ NO

FORMAT ☐ HARDCOVER ☐ PAPERBACK ☐ EBOOK ☐ AUDIOBOOK

SOURCE ☐ BOUGHT ☐ BORROWED ☐ GIFTED ☐ OTHER ______

STARTED SERIES ______

FINISHED SERIES ______

WOULD RECOMMEND?
☐ YES ☐ NO ☐ MAYBE

RECOMMEND TO ______

WOULD READ AGAIN?
☐ YES ☐ NO ☐ MAYBE

WOULD READ OTHER AUTHOR'S BOOKS?
☐ YES ☐ NO ☐ MAYBE

SERIES RATING

EASE OF READING
☆☆☆☆☆

CHARACTERS
☆☆☆☆☆

PLOT
☆☆☆☆☆

ENJOYABILITY
☆☆☆☆☆

OVERALL RATING
☆☆☆☆☆

DESCRIBE THE SERIES IN ONE SENTENCE ______

WHAT DREW ME TO THIS SERIES? ______

QUOTES/FAVORITE PASSAGES ______

REVIEW ______

SERIES REVIEW

#

TITLE	AUTHOR

☐ FICTION
☐ NON-FICTION

GENRE ______

FIRST PUBLISHED ______

BOOKS IN SERIES ______

SERIES COMPLETE? ☐ YES ☐ NO

FORMAT ☐ HARDCOVER ☐ PAPERBACK ☐ EBOOK ☐ AUDIOBOOK

SOURCE ☐ BOUGHT ☐ BORROWED ☐ GIFTED ☐ OTHER ______

DESCRIBE THE SERIES IN ONE SENTENCE

WHAT DREW ME TO THIS SERIES?

QUOTES/FAVORITE PASSAGES

REVIEW

STARTED SERIES

FINISHED SERIES

WOULD RECOMMEND?

☐ YES ☐ NO ☐ MAYBE

RECOMMEND TO

WOULD READ AGAIN?

☐ YES ☐ NO ☐ MAYBE

WOULD READ OTHER AUTHOR'S WORKS?

☐ YES ☐ NO ☐ MAYBE

SERIES RATING

EASE OF READING

☆☆☆☆☆

CHARACTERS

☆☆☆☆☆

PLOT

☆☆☆☆☆

ENJOYABILITY

☆☆☆☆☆

OVERALL RATING

☆☆☆☆☆

NOTES

NOTES

NOTES

NOTES

NOTES

NOTES

NOTES

NOTES

www.ingramcontent.com/pod-product-compliance
Ingram Content Group UK Ltd.
Pitfield, Milton Keynes, MK11 3LW, UK
UKHW020309061125
8793UKWH00004B/592